TAPAS
Barcelona

Foreword **Joan Barril**
Photographs **Jordi García**
Text **Josep Liz**
Recipes **Amanda Laporte**

I0354751

TRIANGLE▼BOOKS

TAPAS
Barcelona

40 Recipes

10 Routes

98

To prepare your own tapas at home, to share with family or friends and show off your skills to make the best tapas from Barcelona. With the advice of expert Amanda Laporte, and following her simple instructions, you can prepare delicious deep-fried potato chunks, *patatas bravas*, Spanish potato salad, cod fritters, deep-fried squid rings, meatballs and cuttlefish, mince and potato balls, Catalan crème brûlée... and up to 40 veggie, fish, seafood, meat or sweet tapas.

180

Every neighbourhood in Barcelona has its own distinctive personality, forged by the passage of time and the neighbours living there. To discover their gastronomic heritage, we bring you these 10 routes to discover the most distinctive tapas bars.

Pepita Napolitana amb mozarella i tomàquets

Mc Pepita amb pa... ...regides

Pepita ...e brut... amb poma caramellizada

Pepita de bu... ...s espàrrecs Pepita

Pepita de ti... ...lmó Bikini

Pepita veg... ...apenade

...el brut Nature -4'5€

...rnil ibèric... ...l'escala: 5'75€ Seitons 3'75€

...va especial... el seitó -2€

...C. (very important croquette)

su tipo de refresco
Pepsi-Cola

la Pepita IZAKAYA ...palates... de bonitol :5€

TARTAR de Salmó ...lada :6€ d'esqueixada -6€
amb shitake :7€ ...e -7€ amb tomàquet :5€

Foie mi-cuit amb -9'8... ...€ ou
xocolata i té vert

Tonyina "soasada" amb miso -9€

Foie a la plancha amb esa...

Pepsi-Cola

The heat of small things

Joan Barril

The act of eating can be simply nutritional or mere pleasure. That's the difference between biology and civilisation, or, what amounts to the same thing, all those aspects that set human beings apart from other animal species. The human race boasts about its ability to do things for its body just because it wants to, and with good reason. That's why you'll find us propping up the bar and having a drink without needing to be thirsty, or expending a great deal of energy on seduction techniques so we can have sex without there being any external circumstances forcing us to do so. The act of eating is no exception, particularly in this world of abundance. We have established set times for the consumption of food. But we have also built a set of rules and trades around food that make life easier for the diner and transform the act of eating into a small celebration: waiters, kitchen boys, maître d's and great chefs, as well as the compilers of recipe books and researchers into our grandmothers' time-honoured cuisines have elevated the act of cooking to a relatively modern science known as "gastronomy". The leading experts in raw

ingredients should also be included in this group: the farmers who bring us the best of the seasons, the butchers who separate the top-quality meat from excellent offal, and the fishermen who take their catch to the fish markets, harvested from a sea that always remains hidden from the land-dweller's gaze. And finally the engineers who have managed to bring something other than heat to the kitchen and created, with their miracle gadgets, delicious emulsions, tinned produce, razor-sharp slices and wedding cakes that make you want to get married over and over again.

This is how the cuisines of the world have been forged. We don't need to know why we have reached this stage or who brought us here. Whether it were an emperor in his gilded dining room or a team of peasant labourers taking a break under a fig tree, the only certainty is that there can be no turning back for the invention of cuisine. Times of shortage and plague may come but we will always retain the memory and stimulus of what we have lost so that we can recover it one day. These lines are a tribute to all those people who have made it possible to replace the endemic hunger in countries of abundance with the democratic pleasure of finding a joyful example of shared human pleasure on the bottom of a plate.

However, this is no fine-dining tome in which the cooks act as academics and serve their delicious dishes dressed up as secret formulas to prevent their competitors from appropriating them. The aim of the book is to provide an explanation in the simplest, freest and, at the same time, most luxurious terms. After all, when

all's said and done, isn't the Spaniard's propensity for eating at odd times, and, whenever possible, in company, a luxury? The tapa is like the bead on a necklace. You need many beads to make the necklace glitter and attain jewellery status. The tapa isn't about the need to eat but about the need to share. There is no solemnity in sampling tapas other than filling our time and our mouths with the flavours that provide the perfect excuse for a glass of wine, a small draught beer and the joy of conversation. In Spain, there are no contracts signed around a plate of tapas; they are a time to take a break from the cut and thrust of daily life. Because tapas are a type of food accessible to everyone, they provide a moment's respite, in collusion with the waiter, which becomes a way of mixing with people and making friends.

Because tapas aren't meant to be eaten alone. Nor are they meant to be experienced when in a bad mood created by obligations. There are time-honoured tapas and brand-new tapas. But there are no copious tapas, because each tapa allows the diners to go Dutch, meaning that everybody sharing in an act that is the closest possible thing to happiness makes the small sacrifice of paying for a round. Going to eat tapas provides official attestation that the time we are about to share will be time well spent. So, let's not fool ourselves. The raw ingredients tapas are made with are not the marinade of the humble olive, or the filling of a tasty omelette, or the pearl-like touch of red mullet caviar, but the extolment of a long-term friendship or the start of a spiritual journey whose destination is unknown.

We do know the origin of tapas as they exist today. History is always written by the powerful. So it comes as no surprise that even a tiny gastronomic titbit like the tapa is attributed to a supposed royal patron: Alfonso X the Wise, the king of Castile. He was suffering from a stomach complaint and his physicians at the court of Toledo advised him to put an immediate halt to the great banquets and binges which the nobility of the time were so fond of, and to restrict his meals to eating little and often. The people soon adopted the fashion established by the sovereign. The monarchs that succeeded him imposed a salutary fine if any tavern or eating house in the Kingdom of Castile failed to serve a free morsel of food with every bowl of wine served to the public. Wine was thought to go down better with a bite to eat, so food was placed over the vessel, like a lid. This is the origin of the word *tapa* (*tapar* is the Spanish verb for *to cover* and *tapa* means *lid*). The food was no more than a mouthful. At most a slice of sausage, a wedge of cheese, or rigid, well-travelled salted fish which made it even more necessary to drink, to the innkeeper's great delight. The custom has endured throughout the centuries without the need for any guidelines or gastronomic codes which, at that time, didn't exactly take into account the health of the royal subjects. Sooner or later, the man in the street would have come to the same conclusion as King Alfonso the Wise did in the 13th century, but that's no reason not to mention the legend attributed to Don Alfonso, a humanist *avant la lettre*.

The centuries went by. And with the fall of the *Ancien Régime*, the castles and palaces lost many members of their kitchen staff. The genius Miguel de Cervantes tells us about this in the first chapter of *Don Quixote* when he describes the knight Alonso Quixano as a man whose diet was in keeping with his penury. In the late 19th century, the former palace cooks began to open smart new restaurants and cafés to cater to the needs of the new bourgeoisie. This phenomenon was widespread in Europe and endures today. However, the Spanish accompaniment par excellence, the tapa, didn't catch on in the rest of the continent, maybe because people weren't aware of its existence or were unaccustomed to it. Here, however, it has undergone constant renewal and the great Spanish chefs have made the field of tapas a way of seeking out the ancestors of popular cuisine that the misnamed *nouvelle cuisine* may have eventually caused to vanish in the hands of the oligopoly of self-appointed artists of the hobs.

Tapas are there to be experienced, so let's move on from the theory. At the present time, in Barcelona, there are many places to eat that are true temples to time-honoured and contemporary tapas. Contrary to all appearances, Barcelona hasn't actually created many home-grown tapas. The secret of their variety is driven by other professionals who have moved here from other parts of Spain. Our local chefs have been dazzled by the success of tapas from the Basque Country, Andalusia, Galicia and Madrid, and have recreated them here. Barcelona has

been a bit slow on the uptake when it comes to absorbing outside influences, as the city's Japanese restaurants, for instance, have shown. However, the end result is wonderful and it's well worth thinking briefly about the different types of tapas the layman can try.

In a hastily put-together classification of tapas it's worth making a distinction between cold and hot tapas. Cold tapas are undoubtedly the earliest form of this type of snack. Stuffed or marinated olives, white or salt-cured anchovies, diced ham or chorizo sausage, blood sausage from Extremadura, ham from the Canary Islands and ham hock from Galicia are just some of the little delicacies that have accompanied Spaniards throughout the centuries. However, hot tapas are more elaborate, but don't actually have to be eaten hot: a nice slice of Spanish or vegetable omelette is a great tapa regardless of the temperature it is served at. In Barcelona, omelette is usually served together with the celebrated *pa amb tomàquet*: a simple combination of a slice of white bread rubbed with tomato, drizzled with olive oil and sprinkled with salt which is nearly always a part of the traditional meals eaten in the city and throughout Catalonia.

We can also make a distinction between dry tapas and mini-casseroles which you can dunk your bread in and mop up the remaining sauce. A dry tapa leaves no trace. It might be a cured *chistorra* sausage from the north, some amazing Padrón peppers, which take their name from the town in Galicia where they are grown,

or the Andalusian wind-dried tuna, *mojama*, which is like tuna ham. The number of tapas you can dip your bread in are as great and varied as the imagination the chef gives rein to by the hotplate. From succulent prawns with garlic to the brutish preparation of tripe and other types of offal. The secret of these tapas is that they never look very filling; they make us reflect on the need for restraint, because this is the only way we'll be able to anticipate the arrival of the better tapa after the good tapa.

There are, of course, ubiquitous tapas and other signature tapas. The ubiquitous ones are already embedded in the collective memory and all we have to do is imitate them so that they become a classic tapa. The most famous are arguably *patatas bravas,* thick chunks of fried potato covered with a mild yet spicy sauce. Russian salad, mussels marinière, tiny shrimps, all kinds of bivalves and those primitive-looking oddities, known as goose barnacles, which are so risky to catch, fit into the group of ubiquitous tapas. In contrast, we find the unique tapas which are the product of the imagination and rigour of specialised cooks who are not so much looking for the confirmation of what has been eaten but information about what we had never imagined eating. The modern tapa is a little marvel of fusion involving different raw ingredients sourced from all the markets of the world and given a Spanish twist, without any qualms. These types of tapas have transcended the bar top and some have even carved a niche for themselves among the aperitifs

and pre-meal snacks served at the top restaurants. They have been a gastronomic way of shifting from *prêt-à-porter* to *haute couture*.

The traditional tapa has two great allies. On the one hand, the natural cycle of the seasons. And, on the other, the preserve or tin. These are the simplest, most cost-effective tapas, because they are usually canned when the market prices are at their lowest. And because storing tapas, conveniently tinned, means we can eat them any time we want. There are also tapas whose very origin entitles them to a passport certifying their nationality. One of Barcelona's genuine, home-grown tapas goes by the name of the *bomba*: a spherical croquette measuring some six centimetres in diameter, filled with mashed potato and topped with a dollop of thick spicy sauce, like those projectiles that were used when the artillery was in its infancy. Just as the popular croissant prides itself on having been created at the bakeries on the day when the Turkish army – whose flag was emblazoned with the crescent moon – finally lifted the siege of Vienna, Barcelona also conjures up, in these delicious *bombas*, the permanent internal squabbles which the Spanish armies took advantage of in an attempt to domesticate the Catalan people by bombing them into submission. Fortunately, ordering a tapa of *bombas* is no longer a hostile act for anyone, but a sociable, fraternal gesture.

While the *bomba* requires the use of a little fork to cut it up, the Basque tradition has brought us the famous *pintxo*, a disposable wooden toothpick which is

CON | 1'80 | CALAMAR | 6'
BAS | 2'10 | PULPO | 3'4
TIFARRA | 3'50 | RECORTES PULPO | 3'4
HORIZO | 3'10 | BACALAO | 5'5
P i POTA | 3'50 | ESCABECHE | 5'0
ANIDA | 2'30 | ESQUEIXADA | 4'5
DIAS | 2'30 | GAMBES | 9'6

used to skewer the tapa. Tapas bars, or *taperías*, have gradually made this practice widespread. Once you've eaten the tapa, you keep the toothpicks on the side of your plate and the owners count them and charge you the same price for each tapa. The *pintxo* has come to Barcelona and it's here to stay.

Now let's get back to our friend and predecessor Alfonso X the Wise. There's no doubt that the point of the tapa was to provide a kind of plump cushion for wine to rest on in our stomachs, so that's why it is essential to talk about wines. The Barcelona tradition has taken refuge in cava. This is a fresh sparkling wine which has been shut away for years – in a cellar, of course – and fermented twice. This fermentation has given it an extra degree of alcohol and a pressure of six atmospheres inside every bottle. In some parts of the city, you'll find cider, a refreshing apple drink, which the guests pour straight from the barrel splashing it on the side of a sturdy glass. There are still people who regularly drink vermouth. In addition to the world's leading brands, there are a good number of bars that claim to make their own vermouth. The problem with vermouth is that it goes to your head and you can't drink too much of it. Beer consumption is on the up and the wines from around country have maintained their rankings. Wine is a great friend of the tapa, but the tapa isn't a great friend of wine. Wine merchants have a highly meaningful saying which has spread to the rest of the Spanish language: *"No me la vayas a dar con queso"* which translates literally as "Don't give it to me with

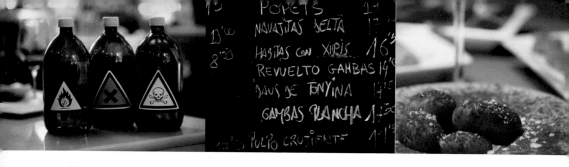

cheese" but means "You can't fool me". This warning originated from the world of innkeepers and producers. Over the years, we have come to realise that cheese improves the flavour of wine. Eating a tapa of cheese is a wonderful exercise, but putting it in the hands of the finest wine in the cellar devalues it. This is not the case with serrano ham, an Iberian product that seems to be crying out for a nice glass of the type of wine that rendered Noah unconscious.

The tapa isn't the most suitable thing for lovers of silence and the contemplative life. Because tapas require company they clearly involve noise. Just as tapas are at odds with solitude, they are also at odds with the armchair. Eating while standing up is an activity more commonly associated with ruminants and armies on the move than diners in formal surroundings. The tapa even seems to act as a spring that keeps us upright next to the plate. Because the tapa doesn't face us; it is always by our side. The tapa doesn't challenge us; it gets involved instead and becomes the focus of conversation, helping us believe that any time spent in its company has made us better on the inside and on the outside. That's the spiritual dimension of something as genuinely material as these little mouthfuls of knowledge for omnivores. Eating together is a way of celebrating life. But pecking at these tiny morsels, as if we were mere migrating birds in search of our own pieces of sky and a memory engraved on our tongues, proves that we're alive and have come here to fill our lives with sensations.

The tapas are ready. Optimism emerges. The explorer's curiosity does the rest. After a Barcelona of tapas, all that remains is to let yourself be transported by Gaudí's mineral spirals and let history slowly rock you with the satisfaction of pleasures fulfilled. ▼

TAPAS
Barcelona

CAÑETE
Catalan cuisine with an Andalusian spirit

José María Parrado has always been at ease working in a kitchen or behind the bar. His parents, Manolo and Mari, moved to Barcelona from Andalusia in 1960, and opened their first bar in Molins de Rei, where José María was born. They later set up another in the blue-collar neighbourhood of La Verneda. It was at these busy local bars, with their good honest food, that José María had his first experience of working in a kitchen when still a small child. Manolo and Mari wanted their son to have a different life and sent him to an elite school in the chicest part of Barcelona, but, as it turned out, a leopard can't change its spots and José María ended up following in his parents' footsteps. Like many young people, he went backpacking around the world, learning languages and working as a parking attendant, kitchen hand and maître, and then returned to Barcelona. In 1998 he opened a successful bar with an outdoor terrace behind the Boqueria Market and went on to launch Cañete in 2010. The bar is located in the Raval district, just a stone's throw away from La Rambla and the opera house, the Gran Teatre del Liceu. In a short space of time it has become one of Barcelona's unmissable places to sample tapas and tasting platters.

Andalusian-style courtyard at the back of Cañete

Eating tapas at Cañete is like going back to the roots of eating side by side at the bar, because that's exactly what this place consists of: a long bar – behind a cosy space with a bistro-like feel that provides a showcase for the excellent home-made desserts – which ends in an Andalusian-style courtyard. And behind the bar, with the stove tops in view, a team of dedicated chefs and waiters tend politely to their customers, guiding them and explaining in detail about the wide variety of tapas and tasting platters on offer.

The kitchen is supervised by Juanba Agreda who has proved to be the perfect ally for Parrado to bring his project to fruition: Catalan-Andalusian fusion cooking where the integrity of the produce, skills, classicism and most current techniques come first. It's not easy to choose, but during your first visit, you must try the fried marinated fish; the anchovies from Santoña in olive oil; the sea anemones from Chipiona; the acorn-fed ham croquettes and the sweetbreads with red prawns, wild mushrooms and meat juices. And don't forget the delicious desserts, such as the Cuban chocolate stick with salt, soft cheese cake with pear and the *torrijas* (Spanish pain perdu) with communion wine. You can wash them all down with a glass of handpulled Moritz beer or choose from the excellent wine list which features more than 150 different wines, 30 of them available by the glass. Step inside, eat and enjoy!

FÀBRICA MORITZ
Barcelona's brewery

Since the middle of 2012, Fàbrica Moritz has been a temple dedicated to the worship of beer, a gastronomic, cultural and recreational hub and one of Europe's largest microbreweries. It also has a concept store with a Triticum bakery, a newsstand, a stall selling fresh, unpasteurised beer and a section with designer objects. They are all housed inside a vast, spectacular space that was home to the original Moritz brewery. Moritz first opened in 1864 and the building has undergone a major refit undertaken by the prestigious architect Jean Nouvel to mark this new chapter in its history.

And because everything here is large in scale – from the opening times (the Fàbrica Moritz opens from 6am to 3am) to the beautiful metal-clad bar which is 26 m long, the backlit panels with the brand logo and the gigantic copper stills which work endlessly to produce the fresh beer – you'll find a menu featuring more than 300 dishes.

Jordi Vilà at Fàbrica Moritz

The chef Jordi Vilà (who earned one Michelin star at his restaurant Alkimia) is at the helm and has opted for a cuisine that brings together regions as far apart as Catalonia and Alsace (the homeland of the brewery founder Louis Moritz) and also includes typical Andalusian fried platters, Galician-style seafood, German sausages and cold cuts, and French-style *cocottes*. A magnificent culinary panorama where you'll be spoilt for choice, although here are a few suggestions: battered monkfish with tartare sauce served on a bed of chicory; octopus; crisp-fried squid rings; crunchy ham croquettes; spicy bravas "from round here"; mini frankfurter made from artisan *Nürnberger* sausage; *coca de recapte* flatbread topped with grilled vegetables and a baby sardine in olive oil; *Flammkuchen* (a traditional Alsatian fine pizza base with a variety of toppings); sauerkraut with artisan sausages; and poussin à la Moritz with chips.

And, of course, because Jordi Vilà began his career at the age of 15 at the Baixas patisserie and was named top pastry chef in 2006, you'll have to leave room for his *bunyols de l'Empordà* (anise-flavoured sugar-coated fritters), the crème brûlée, the peach gazpacho with yoghurt and orange, and the dark chocolate fondant pot. And to drink, although there are many other options – the Fàbrica Moritz has an excellent cellar with 400 types of wine and a special selection of French and Alsatian wines – don't miss out on the opportunity to sample some of the fresh, unpasteurised beers from the microbrewery. Fàbrica Moritz: beer-inspired dishes at "the place to beer"!

CATALAN AND ALSATIAN CUISINE AT EUROPE'S LARGEST MICROBREWERY, THE FORMER PREMISES OF THE ORIGINAL MORITZ BREWERY (1864) REMODELED BY JEAN NOUVEL.

LA PEPITA
The female version is better

Why is the female version better? You'll need to try it to be convinced and applaud what Sofia Boixet and Sergio Andreu have done: they have given a female twist to the popular, common-or-garden pork loin sandwich, known in Spanish as a *pepito de lomo* and turned it into an exquisite delicacy that comes in a whole host of varieties, including fish, placed between two crunchy, delicate and wafer-thin slices of bread. And what did they decide to call this delicacy – and, by extension, their bar? Pepita, of course, after their grandmothers who were both fine exponents of good home cooking.

But La Pepita doesn't live on *pepita* sandwiches alone. Sergio Andreu, an industrial designer with an academic background, recognised his true vocation in the culinary arts. After a spell at the cookery school run by the one-Michelin-starred restaurant Hofmann, he moved to Paris with Sofia to work for two years in the kitchens of El Fogón, the restaurant run by the chef Alberto Herraiz where Parisians can enjoy the finest Spanish tapas.

Sergio Andreu preparing a *pepita*

Sofia Boixet and Sergio Andreu behind the bar of La Pepita

When the young couple returned to Barcelona in December 2010, they opened La Pepita in the neighbourhood of Gràcia which borders on the Eixample district just a stone's throw away from its main thoroughfare, the majestic Passeig de Gràcia. The bar is suffused with the Catalan and Mediterranean spirit but also has some touches that are reminders of the time they spent in the French capital. The dado which replicates the tiles at the Odéon metro station – which used to be "their" station – is a good example of this. Customers can write, draw or graffiti messages on the tiles to add a touch of colour, which is different every time you visit the bar.

But let's go back to what is important. In addition to the *pepitas*, La Pepita serves a wide variety of classic tapas "turbocharged" with Sergio's incisive creative touch – accompanied by a cooling glass of handpulled Estrella Damm beer or wine served by the glass which you can choose from the extensive wine list – served by attentive, friendly and highly professional staff. You have to try the Russian salad, the *Very Important* Croquette, the anchovy with dulce de leche, the chicken croquettes on a bed of romesco sauce, the white anchovy with black olive jam and the "tapalatas" – tapas served in tins which remind us of traditional Spanish tinned preserved foods – of foie mi-cuit and *esqueixada de bacallà* (shredded salt cod salad). And you have to leave room for the wonderful desserts, such as the light and delicate *crema catalana* and, Sofia's favourite, the amazing curd cheese with mead. A culinary round of applause for La Pepita!

CLASSIC TAPAS "TURBOCHAR-GED" WITH SERGIO'S CREATIVE TOUCH AT THIS BAR WITH A PARISIAN FEEL.

29

ELS TRES PORQUETS
A culinary tale with a happy ending

Just like the traditional folk tale (*Els Tres Porquets* is *The Three Little Pigs* in Catalan), Marc Cuenca's culinary initiative has a happy ending, particularly for the diners who step inside this tiny eatery with its décor midway between a French bistro and a Madrid tavern.

Marc studied telecommunications engineering but was born and raised in the kitchen and at the tables of Can Pineda, a small, old-style restaurant in the Clot district where its wonderful food has been enjoyed by those in the know for 40 years. When the time came for him to find a job, he chose to follow the family tradition and opened Els Tres Porquets, where he works as head waiter and sommelier: another type of "engineering" that is equally communicative. Roger Boronat, who trained at Can Pineda, is in charge of the kitchen.

Marc Cuenca writes the tapas menu on the blackboard

And while we're on the subject of the kitchen, Els Tres Porquets serves truly succulent, traditional dishes made with market-fresh ingredients. Seasonal produce takes centre stage and is treated with loving care and skill. If you want to find out for yourself, after you've had a tapa of Guijuelo Iberico ham or anchovies washed down with a small glass of handpulled Mahou beer, you have to try the tomato medley with tuna belly; the Maresme peas in their juices; tuna cubes with lime and soy sauce; the crispy octopus with potato puree and paprika oil; the duck egg with morels and foie gras; the truffle risotto; the meatballs with wild mushrooms; and the meat stew, *alambre*. Served in half portions, they are perfect for sharing, so the more dishes you order from the menu the better. You can't leave Els Tres Porquets without trying the desserts. Highlights include the amazing chocolate *bombe* and the excellent *recuit* (curd cheese) from Fonteta with honey from Rioja.

You can pair the dishes with one of 400 fine wines from around the world featured on the iPad wine list. Not for nothing is this small eatery one of Barcelona's top wine bars. And if you want to linger at the table after your meal, why not order a gin and tonic? This is another speciality of the house and you can choose from 34 gins featured on the iPad menu. And what about the wolf? He was happy too at Els Tres Porquets!

MOUTH-WATERING CUISINE WHICH UPDATES THE CULINARY TRADITIONS OF CAN PINEDA IN THIS SMALL BISTRO-STYLE TAVERN.

GRAN BODEGA SALTÓ
A triumph of romanticism

Few traditional bodegas survive in Barcelona, a city that shows little gratitude towards its centuries-old emporiums. However, fate often imitates the screenplays of Frank Capra's films. So when José Luis Cánovas and Lidia López entered the Saltó for the first time to buy a bottle of cava on 31st December 2001 to celebrate New Year's Eve, they fell hopelessly in love with the place. However, their joy at the discovery soon turned to disappointment and sadness when the owner told them that the bodega was going to close down on 15th January. And this is where our central characters turned their dose of romanticism to their advantage. How else can we explain why a teacher on temporary leave and a salesman nicknamed "the Tiger" because he played in La Ruge Band in his spare time ("ruge" is Spanish for "roar"), who had no kind of experience in the world of catering, decided to take over the bar to prevent it from being forgotten like so many others?

Décor midway between kitsch and naïf at this unique bodega

José Luis Cánovas at the entrance to his bodega

Well, La Gran Bodega Saltó has neither been forgotten nor abandoned. Today it plays a pivotal role in the Poble-sec neighbourhood's rich community life, and hosts concerts in support of the local residents. It is a meeting place for musicians, painters, poets, actors and all kinds of bohemians and has become the flagship for the revival of Poble-sec as one of the city's liveliest neighbourhoods. Ample proof of this was given when it was awarded the Time Out prize for Barcelona's best night-time bar in 2012.

At the start of their venture, José Luis and Lidia joined forces with the British artist Steven Forster, who created a spectacular intervention among the original kegs and barrels entitled "cambiar todo sin cambiarlo del todo" (change everything without changing everything about it). An explosive burst of colours drawing on his personal world, between the kitsch and naïf, on sculptures, mobiles, lamps and walls which are decorated with drawings and phrases about wine, as well as the magnificent, sinuous bar, which features lines from one of the Bacchanalian poems from *Carmina Burana*.

And to end with, an excellent culinary offering consisting of cold tapas of Iberico acorn-fed ham, Boffard and Manchego cheeses, and fresh and cured anchovies or cod which if ordered as tiny mouthfuls or "bocaditos" become an irresistible temptation: fresh and cured anchovies on squid ink bread, white tuna with piquillo peppers on green-olive bread, salt cod carpaccio and olive paste on tomato bread, and Iberico acorn-fed pork loin on dark-beer bread. Excellent wines, some of them served from the barrel, delicious Estrella de Galicia beer and great vermouth on tap complete an experience that is as unique as it is unforgettable. Gran Bodega Saltó: the Tiger roars!

GRAN BODEGA SALTÓ
Carrer de Blesa, 36 ▸ Route **5**

EXCELLENT RANGE OF COLD TAPAS CONSISTING OF IBERICO HAMS, SELECT CHEESES AND TINNED FISH.

TEN'S TAPAS RESTAURANT
The simplicity of haute cuisine

It is said that youth is intrepid, audacious and unfazed by anything, and can even be reckless and impetuous. This may be why Jordi Cruz was bold enough to present himself as a chef at the tender age of 14. He may not have been skilled in his trade at the time but he certainly knew which direction he wanted to take: he had wanted to be a chef since the age of seven. Was it just intuition? No way! Put simply. He was very good at cooking and very bad at everything else. And the gamble paid off: at the age of 17 he was already a head chef and at the age of 24 was awarded his first Michelin star, making him the youngest chef in Spain and the second in the world to receive this accolade.

However, his journey to "stardom" didn't stop there and in just under ten years he has garnered four of them. He was awarded one star at the Estany Clar, in Cercs, and another at L'Angle in Sant Fruitós de Bages – which is currently located in the Hotel Cram in Barcelona – followed by Àbac – one of the city's temples of haute cuisine – which holds two. Jordi Cruz's venture into the world of tapas remains consistent with his career as a self-taught chef and his personal idea of cutting-edge cuisine that transcends fashions and trends and is now applied to one of the humblest areas of gastronomy: tapas and small platters of food.

Jordi Cruz in the Ten's

Neo-rationalist entrance to Ten's

It goes by the name of Ten's and is situated in the Born district, on the ground floor of the Park Hotel, an interesting neo-rationalist building designed by the architect Antoni de Moragas dating from 1953. In addition to its two welcoming terraces, Ten's has a simple, open-plan interior decorated with extraordinary taste in keeping with the building's original architectural features and far removed from clichéd Spanish bars. As soon as the customers arrive, they immediately feel at home because they don't have to jostle for space as they would have to do in other tapas bars, and they receive friendly, efficient service.

Jordi Cruz sets out to make tapas more dignified and free of any pretentions by using top-quality produce as the key ingredient. Tapas and small servings you can share which show a creativity that respects the finest tapas tradition while taking it to another level: *patatas bravas* (deep-fried potato wedges) with an aioli foam and spicy sofrito sauce; Cantabrian anchovies on toast with tomato and creamed black garlic; Andalusian-style calamari cone with lemon grass aioli; egg cooked at a low temperature with ceps, Jerusalem artichoke, Parmesan and truffle; cooked octopus sprinkled with smoked paprika served on a beechwood-smoked potato with arbequina olive oil; or chargrilled Iberico pork rib meat and tail with honeyed sweet potato mash are just some of the unmissable suggestions on your first visit. You should also leave room for one of the delicious desserts such as the rice and coconut pudding with yoghurt and lemon ice cream, or the apple tarte Tatin with curd cheese and honey ice cream. All of them washed down with that enjoyable, rough diamond of drinks that is a favourite accompaniment for tapas: a glass of handpulled Estrella Damm beer. Ten's, humble tapas brought to the high altar of haute cuisine.

TEN'S TAPAS RESTAURANT
Carrer del Rec, 79 ► Route **2**

CRUZ SETS OUT TO MAKE
TAPAS MORE DIGNIFIED IN
KEEPING WITH HIS CAREER AS
A SELF-TAUGHT CHEF AND HIS
PERSONAL IDEA OF CUTTING-
EDGE CUISINE.

LOLITA TAPERIA
Stay in the loop

This is what Joan Martínez has managed to do. The determined and passionate proprietor masterminded the transformation of the Inopia Classic Bar into Lolita Taperia: a must-visit bar if you don't want to be out of the tapas loop.

Joan Martínez and Albert Adrià are childhood friends and schoolmates who decided to set up a "typical" bar where all the tapas were "atypical", not just the occasional one, as was the case in the bars in the working class neighbourhood of Santa Eulàlia where they used to spend their time when they bunked off school. This is how Inopia came about in 2006. Along with Tapas 24, it shares the honour of being one of the first gastro bars in Barcelona. In 2010, following four years' success and the amicable dissolution of the Adrià-Martínez partnership, Joan tackled the renovation and renewal of the bar with his customary enthusiasm and it reopened the same year.

A lipstick mark defines the image of Lolita

Joan Martínez inside his tapas bar

A threefold renewal: in the interior design, with its energetic and colourful yet simple decor; in its name, which includes a reference to tapas and introduces a woman's name which is very popular in Spain and reminiscent of Nabokov around the world; and in the kitchen. Although Lolita still serves some of the "classics" from Inopia, it includes new creations, with chef Xavier Castillo at the helm. Standing on a street corner in the Sant Antoni neighbourhood, Lolita is now a bar, a *vermuteria*, restaurant, bistrot and watering hole.

To begin with, order a refreshing glass of Moritz (the neighbourhood beer) and the crispy *pa de vidre* flatbread, followed by the wind-dried red tuna, the air-dried Wagyu beef, Iberico ham, or the Russian salad with crunchy mini breadsticks, baby broad beans with truffle, avocado and quail egg, and the battered squid rings in a cone. And you can continue with a glass of Catalan wine or cava – recommended by Joan – and some of the Inopia classics: aubergines with molasses, spicy potato chunks (*patatas bravas*), the Iberico ham croquettes, the chicken strips (deep fried in a special potato-crisp crumb) and the fried fish. You must try the open-topped sandwiches known as "Puces de Vidre" (served on a crunchy slice of bread, they include the Quimet which has a topping of salmon, Greek yoghurt and truffle honey, and the De la Costa – the "one from the coast" – featuring sardines), or the classic sandwiches, such as the mini burger and the Don Pepito. And to end with, the desserts, of course: the Fonteta curds, pineapple with lime zest and sugar molasses, the Lolita tipsy cake and the home-made crème caramel, one of Joan's favourites. Welcome to Lolita, mwah, mwah!

LOLITA TAPERIA
Carrer de Tamarit, 104 ▸ Route **6**

THE RENEWAL OF LOLITA AFTER INOPIA CLASSIC BAR CLOSED REMAINS TRUE TO THE CULINARY CHALLENGE IN AN INFORMAL, FRIENDLY ATMOSPHERE.

LA VINYA DEL SENYOR
The Wine Bar of the Sea or the Cathedral of Wine

La Vinya del Senyor opened in 1998 in one of the most beautiful spots in Barcelona's medieval quarter. This small and beautiful bar with its spacious terrace stands opposite the Gothic basilica of Santa Maria del Mar, which is known as the "Cathedral of the Sea". La Vinya was founded by Ramon Parellada – a member of one of Catalonia's oldest and longest restaurant dynasties: seven generations who have run iconic restaurants such as the Fonda Europa, in Granollers, or the restaurant Senyor Parellada in the neighbouring Carrer de la Argenteria – and Quim Vila, one of the country's leading wine authorities who runs Vila Viniteca – a veritable shrine for wine buffs – in the nearby Carrer dels Agullers. It stocks more than 5000 wines from all over the world and from different designations of origin.

Entrance to the Vinya del Senyor

This may be why La Vinya (the Catalan for "vineyard") takes a radical stance when it comes to drinks, in spite of the proverb "You'll find everything in the vineyard of the Lord". It's not a place for beer drinkers, or people looking for a soft drink: you won't find them here. La Vinya is one of the city's best wine bars, with more than 350 wines from around the world, 20 of them available by the glass. These 20 varieties change every fortnight meaning that lovers of fine wines can further their tasting knowledge.

The tapas and small servings, created under the supervision of Fermí Puig, are designed to match any kind of wine to perfection: white, rosé, red, sparkling... and are made with top-quality artisan produce. The warm tapa highlights include the smoked-oil potatoes with La Vera paprika, the cannelloni made from roast meat and boletus oil, and the croquettes; and if you fancy some cold tapas, you simply must try the *puces* – small olive oil bread buns served with Iberico ham, Minorcan sobrassada sausage, spicy chorizo from Astorga or Pico Melero cheese, among other ingredients. You can also sample the fresh seasonal oysters, the Pallars secallona sausage and the wind-dried toro tuna with almonds. La Vinya del Senyor: ¡In vino veritas!

THE TAPAS AND SMALL SERVINGS ARE DESIGNED TO MATCH ANY KIND OF WINE TO PERFECTION.

EL VELÓDROMO
A second childhood

This is what the legendary El Velódromo has been enjoying since it reopened in 2009 with Moritz – Barcelona's brewery par excellence since 1856 – at the helm. If you want to understand why the bar is so legendary you have to go back to 1933 when it first opened and soon became a meeting place for Barcelona's intellectuals during the tumultuous years of that decade: members of the Republican government who had been exiled to Barcelona following the capture of Madrid by Franco's troops. Over the years, the bar became one of the fiefdoms of the left and, during the long years of the dictatorship, clandestine meetings took place around its tables where the famous tram drivers' strike of 1951, among other events, were planned. Following its closure in the year 2000, when its proprietor and founder Manuel Pastor Boné retired, Moritz Barcelona bought the premises and set about injecting them with new life. The restoration project has retained the classical, art deco style the Velódromo had when it opened and preserved the most visible, characteristic elements of the original design: the large staircase with its mahogany banisters, the cornices, the mirrored shelves behind the bar, the original 1930s' billiard table and many of the original furnishings.

The restoration of the Velódromo has retained the classical, art deco style of 1933

The mirrored shelves behind the array of tapas on the bar

The food on offer also had to reflect the special charm of the bar and there was no one better to take on the challenge than chef Jordi Vilà (who had obtained one Michelin star at his restaurant Alkimia), who made a firm commitment to Catalan cuisine with a French twist in the style of the classic bistros: unfussy dishes consisting of tapas and small servings with the democratic purpose of satisfying any palate. The kitchen opens from 6am to 3am every day.

In addition to the "tapas de barra" (fresh and cured anchovies; *banderillas* (olives, red peppers, cocktail onions and anchovies on a stick) and *gildas* (the same combination but with the addition of a green jalapeño pepper), the Velódromo is also renowned for its cooked tapas which you can dip your bread in. These include the *Siscentó* Barcelona (aubergine, roasted vegetable salad and anchovy); the squid rings in batter; the *bomba de la Barceloneta* (giant beef and potato croquette served with a spicy *brava* sauce and alioli); the *esqueixada* (shredded salt cod salad); fried eggs with Perol sausage; the macaroni au gratin; the squid rice; and the veal cheeks in Epidor beer.

Moving on to the desserts, you'll find classics such as the giant rum baba with cane rum, the *crema catalana* and the cheese crème caramel with a crumble topping, as well as home-made cakes, including the Sacher torte and tarte tatin. And to drink it has to be hand-pulled Moritz beer, served in small or large glasses. If you're in the mood, you can always choose one of the "21-hour Non-Stop Cocktails": fixed-price cocktails at any time of day. Gastronomic pleasure in a cosmopolitan atmosphere!

MUNDIAL BAR
A century in El Born

Francesc Tort, the present owner of this iconic, authentic and successful bar, can trace the family tradition back to the time of his grandfather, Miquel, who, at the age of 16, in 1914, rented the Bodega la Chispa where he was working as a waiter. In 1925, Miquel decided to change the name of the bodega and call it the Bar Mundial, a name more in keeping with the times ("mundial" means "worldly" in Catalan) when the city and the neighbourhood were in the throes of major changes: Barcelona was getting ready for the 1929 International Exhibition, and the central food market, El Born, and the Estació de França, the railway station connecting Barcelona and Europe, were the main engines of economic activity which brought in visitors and workers from all over Spain.

The aesthetics of the bar remain faithful to its history: terrazzo floors, tiled walls, marble-topped tables with wrought-iron legs and walls covered with boxing memorabilia. Behind the bar there are photographs signed by the boxers of the day and, on the wall opposite, there is a huge collage also featuring boxers.

The walls of the Mundial preserve the bar's "pugilistic" past

The Tort family at the entrance to the Mundial

Fortunately, this décor has survived. The boxing connection is the result of the friendship Miquel struck up with the bullfighting and boxing promoter Pedro Balañá in 1938 when the Bar Mundial became the headquarters of the Segundo Bartos' supporters' club (Bartos was Spanish lightweight boxing champion in 1933 and 1934). The club broke up in 1965, but its memory endures on the walls of the Mundial.

However, the tapas and small servings are not just a memory… they are a reality and are served to a clientele who are more "worldly" than ever. For the past 35 years, the tapas and small servings at the Mundial have included fresh seafood and fish and other market-fresh ingredients, first under the culinary baton of Francesc's mother and aunt and later under Andrés Rosillo. You can still enjoy the preserves and pickles the Mundial has served since it first opened.

Francesc recommends a glass of house vermouth or a small Estrella Damm draught beer, depending on the time of day, to go with your tapas, although, if you prefer, they also serve wine by the glass or the bottle. He also suggests you try the tuna, prawn and crab salad, the squid rings in batter, the griddled cockles and razor clams, the cuttlefish with meatballs, the finely sliced aubergines with honey and goat's cheese, the Catalan-style salt cod – *bacallà a la llauna* –, the tenderloin with red berries and fresh foie gras, cuttlefish strips with truffles flambéed in rum, and fresh tuna with tomato and mint. And for dessert, the white and dark chocolate fondant, the mojito mousse, the lime and mango cake and the orange Sacher torte. There's a saying in Catalan that goes *Roda el món i torna al Born* (which means something like "you may travel the world but you'll always come home"). You may travel the world but you'll always come back to the Mundial!

MUNDIAL BAR
Plaça de Sant Agustí Vell, 1 ▸ Route **2**

FISH AND SEAFOOD (PARTICU-
LARLY SHELLFISH) ARE THE
SPECIALITIES YOU MUST TRY
TO CAPTURE THE ESSENCE
OF THE MUNDIAL.

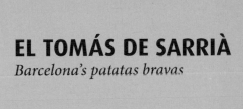

EL TOMÁS DE SARRIÀ

Barcelona's patatas bravas

In Barcelona, El Tomás is synonymous with the fried potato chunks known as *patatas bravas*. El Tomás has stood on the main street in the district of Sarrià since 1919 although the current bar stands opposite the original premises and dates from 1956. It has the same bar, windows and furnishings from the time. During its first half century, El Tomás was a typical neighbourhood bodega that sold wine from the barrel, fizzy drinks, beers and soft drinks and a place where you could also have a tinned tapa.

In the early 1970s, the owners, who hail from Aragon, began to serve *patatas bravas*. They enjoyed spectacular success and their fame spread beyond the bar to the rest of the city and the whole country. Today, the *patatas bravas* at El Tomás are world famous.

Diners enjoying the *patatas bravas*

The secret lies in the variety of the potato, the same used to make chips by the friers at the typical fritter stalls and bars known as *churrerías*; in the way they are cut: lengthways into thick, irregular chunks; in the way they are fried to order; and in their texture: crisp and golden on the outside, light and fluffy on the inside. And, of course, the secret key ingredient: the red, very spicy sauce.

In addition to the spicy *bravas* you can also order a plate of *bravas mixtas*, which aren't as hot and are served with a silky smooth aioli. And although there is always a long queue for the *bravas* – there are people waiting in the street half an hour before opening time, particularly at weekends – El Tomás is a tapas bar and customers can sample a wide variety accompanied by a refreshing San Miguel draught beer. The tapas on offer include the white tuna with piquillo pepper served on a cocktail stick, the Cantabrian anchovies, the Russian salad, the home-made chicken croquettes and the white tuna mini pasties.

Although El Tomás isn't as glamorous as other bars, and perhaps because of this, it attracts a diverse clientele of all ages and backgrounds. Here you can mingle with renowned political and cultural figures, young students, workers, local residents or executives and entrepreneurs. They all have a good reason to make their pilgrimage. Tomás: bravo for your *bravas*!

EL TOMÁS DE SARRIÀ
Carrer Major de Sarrià, 49

ALTHOUGH EL TOMÁS OFFERS A WIDE VARIETY OF DISHES, IT WAS CATAPULTED TO WORLDWIDE FAME BY ITS *PATATAS BRAVAS*.

TAPAS, 24
A typical, time-honoured "tavern"

Talking about Carles Abellan, who earned a Michelin star at his restaurant Comerç, 24, is like talking about an obsession: to raise the profile and improve the quality of cuisine in every sphere, even the most modest, according to his own concept of "Barcelona cuisine". He developed this culinary philosophy at the beachfront bar, La Guingueta de la Barceloneta (2013); at the informal eaterie Suculent (2012), which is reminiscent of typical Spanish cheap eateries; at Bravo 24 (2009), where the produce is key and goes back to the roots of cuisine; and at the tapas bar, Tapas, 24 (2006).

These achievements follow a long professional career which began at the Barcelona Catering Academy – he was among the academy's first intake of students – and includes such stimulating experiences as working at elBulli with Ferran Adrià in the 1990s, making his first forays as a chef at the legendary Talaia Mar, where he eventually became manager, and creating the menu with Ferran Adrià for the Hotel Hacienda Benazuza in Seville.

Carles Abellan on the terrace of his bar

While working at this frenetic pace he had time to think about opening his own restaurant and the first project, Comerç, 24, saw the light in 2001. It was named after the street and the number where it is situated in the district of El Born and reflects his own personal concept which had been clear in his mind for some time: signature cuisine in miniature; small servings to which he applied all his creative talents, contemporary in appearance but in the setting of a classic restaurant with a wine list, wine waiter, etc. The restaurant earned him a Michelin star in 2007.

According to Carles Abellan, Tapas, 24 represented a downshifting to the world of traditional tapas, to the time-honoured "tavern", to the tapas we all know and love, while retaining the spirit of Comerç, 24. The first tapas bar to be opened by a Michelin-starred fine-dining chef became a runaway success overnight. If you want to see for yourself, just order the Russian salad with mini breadsticks, the chicken wings with Korean sauce, the trademark pork ribs, the Shunka-style tuna, the Iberico ham or roast chicken croquettes, the Mcfoie-burger and the toasted ham and cheese sandwich, the Bikini Comerç, 24. The chef will advise you on which wine to choose, from a red Abellan Arribas Priorat, to a white Abellan Costers del Segre. For dessert you can choose from chocolate with bread, olive oil and salt, the *crema catalana* or the *carquinyolis*, a type of biscotti biscuit served with a thick slab of chocolate. Tapas, 24, a very successful neighbourhood bar in the heart of Barcelona's Eixample district.

EL XAMPANYET - CA L'ESTEVE
Three generations with one destiny

To make Ca l'Esteve (the Catalan for Steve's place) into a top-of-the-league classic in the city with a "second-division" drink: *xampanyet* sparkling wine. Indeed, since 1929, three generations of Esteves – Esteve Ninou, the founder; Estevet, his son who has been running the business since the mid 1970s; and Joan Carles (who is known by the people in the neighbourhood as "Little Estevet"), the grandson who is keeping the dynasty going – have managed to keep their bar on Carrer Montcada among the city's favourite tapas haunts. And all this in spite of the continuous and substantial changes that have taken place in the neighbourhood of La Ribera.

In 1929, Barcelona's central food market, known as El Born (the name adopted by the entire neighbourhood) was the city's main economic powerhouse. Local commerce consisted of small stores and grocer's shops that supplied the working class population who lived there, and a few cheap restaurants and bodegas that helped make more bearable the little free time the market workers enjoyed.

Estevet at the entrance to El Xampanyet

Following a number of years in the doldrums after the market had moved to the outskirts of the city, El Born has become one of Barcelona's coolest neighbourhoods. It is the area most visited by tourists and visitors of all kinds due to its first-rate cultural attractions (headed by the Museu Picasso and Born Centre Cultural), and a whole host of fashion and designer boutiques run by independent designers from throughout Europe, together with countless restaurants and nighttime bars which have superseded the traditional shops.

Ca l'Esteve has withstood all these changes and its fame has crossed borders. What is the key? To remain true to its style – a typical 1940s' multicoloured, chaotic décor, with mosaic-clad walls, dozens of traditional objects, wine barrels and marble-topped tables with an iron base – and produce: excellent tinned tapas, sausages and cold cuts and salted meat and fish, with particular mention going to the anchovies, which are perhaps the best in the city. Well, there has been a change. The sign above the door has given pride of place to its star drink: *xampanyet*, a sparkling white wine.

Although it may be packed to overflowing, don't hesitate to step inside (the service is fast and efficient and you'll soon find room) and order some of the excellent Cantabrian anchovies (kept in brine in barrels for more than a year, then rinsed and seasoned to perfection with the secret house dressing), the clams, the cockles, the white tuna belly, the mussels in an escabeche pickle and small platters of Iberico cured sausage.

And to drink, you've got to order a glass of *xampanyet*, of course, although if you prefer you can have the house vermouth or a small hand-pulled Estrella Damm beer. El Xampanyet, the most popular place in El Born!

EL XAMPANYET - CA L'ESTEVE
Carrer de Montcada, 22 ▶ Route **2**

EL XAMPANYET, KNOWN TO LOCALS AS CA L'ESTEVE, PROBABLY SERVES THE BEST ANCHOVIES IN BARCELONA.

LA COVA FUMADA
The essence of La Barceloneta

La Cova is synonymous with La Barceloneta, a neighbourhood of blue-collar workers, sailors and fishermen which still retains many of the trademark features it had when it was built on land reclaimed from the sea in the middle of the 18th century. La Cova is a fine example of these. It has been in the neighbourhood since 1945, and is so well known that it doesn't need a sign above the door. The bar goes by the same name the locals gave the previous one that that stood on the site. With its coal-fired ovens that blackened the ceilings and walls, it was known as La Cova Fumada, which means "smoky cave" in Catalan.

Maria Pla and Magí Solé (the grandparents of the current owners, Magí and Josep Maria) opened a bodega in 1945. It had a cheap oven to heat up the food the workers from La Vulcano and La Maquinista (legendary factories in the neighbourhood, now gone), the workers from the quayside, the central fish market and muleteers carried in their lunchboxes.

Palmira Fresquet, Magí and Josep Maria's mother, has continued the culinary traditions of La Cova

Gradually, the grandmother Maria and her son Magí began serving dishes such as sardines and anchovies in escabeche pickle or on the griddle. When they proved successful, they expanded their range of food to include baked salt cod (*bacallà a la llauna*), griddled clams, pig's trotters... However, the dish that catapulted them to fame beyond the boundaries of the neighbourhood was Maria's invention of a potato croquette filled with meat, coated in breadcrumbs and fried, and seasoned with a very spicy sauce invented by her son Magí. It was appropriately named a *bomba* ("bomb" in Catalan).

The founders' grandchildren, Magí and Josep Maria, have worked in La Cova since they were little and, together with Guillem, the fourth generation of the Solé dynasty, retain the essence of the bar, where the counter, tables and atmosphere are the same as they were 70 years ago. The kitchen has kept its faithful admirers while creating new regular customers. Without forgetting the essential *bomba*, you have to try the artichokes, the stewed head and leg of pork (*cap i pota*), the *bacallà a la llauna*, the blood sausage with chick peas (*aixafada*) and, of course, the fish and seafood tapas which, thanks to the owners' lifelong contacts, are brought in fresh from the fish markets in Barcelona and Vilanova: excellent griddled squid, sardines, mussels, razor clams, prawns and langoustines, as well as the octopus marinière and the octopus offcuts with onion. You can accompany the tapas with a glass of house wine (white or red) or a bottle of Estrella Damm beer, served in "quintos" (small 20 cl. bottles) or "mitjanes" (33 cl. bottles). La Cova is the "bomb"!

LA COVA FUMADA RETAINS
THE INDELIBLE ESSENCE
OF LA BARCELONETA:
BARCELONA'S FISHERMEN'S
AND SAILORS' QUARTER.

LA TAVERNA DEL CLÍNIC

The tapas clinic or Epicure's tavern

Don't be fooled by the sign above the door: it's not the soulless cafeteria belonging to the nearby Hospital Clínic (hence the name) or a run-of-the-mill bar with a long counter, cured hams hanging from the ceiling, wine barrels on the walls and the chatter of the regulars ringing in the air.

The tapas, small platters and half portions are prepared with the precision and efficiency of the surgeons at the Hospital Clínic, in a peaceful atmosphere with exquisite interior design, and the "patients" (diners who are a lucky few, given the Taverna's small interior) are offered the "results of surgery" with the same philosophy as Epicure: to provide pleasure in a sensible way, avoiding any excess that may cause subsequent complaints. Put in a nutshell, since 2006, the culinary strengths of La Taverna del Clínic have been concealed behind its somewhat ambiguous and humble name.

These strengths come as no surprise. The young chef, Toni Simoes, who was named best young chef in Catalonia in 2014 by the Catalan Academy of Gastronomy and Nutrition, first worked in a kitchen at the age of 14 at his father's Galician restaurant, O Enxebre. After studying at the Barcelona Cookery School, he finished his training in the kitchen of Can Fabes, the much-missed Santi Santamaría's legendary three-Michelin-starred restaurant. The family's Galician roots and Toni's personal career are reflected in classic dishes given a contemporary twist through creative good judgement and radical produce: biodynamic vegetables, fish straight from local markets and ingredients from small-holdings and allotments. Toni's eldest brother, Manuel Simoes, left the world of industrial and haute-couture pattern design to "design" relations with the customers: he is head waiter at La Taverna del Clínic and an expert sommelier who has earned distinctions such as the Chevalier de l'Ordre de Coteaux de Champagne.

So let Manuel guide you through the menu to find the perfect wine to partner the famous, prize-winning *bravas de la Taverna* (fried potato chunks with a spicy sauce), the octopus igloo, the scallop carpaccio with spinach and yuzu foam, the griddled squid with Jerusalem artichokes and trout caviar, Galician variegated scallops with sake-confit creamed cauliflower and Iranian caviar, the wild mushroom and foie-gras cannelloni, the roll of boned kid stuffed with sweetbreads, and the oxtail timbale in Priorat wine. You can end with an apple tarte tatin or the Todochoco with Macallan whisky. La Taverna del Clínic, culinary epicureanism!

LA TAVERNA DEL CLÍNIC
Carrer del Rosselló, 155 ▶ Route **7**

THE CULINARY STRENGTHS OF THE TAVERNA DEL CLÍNIC ARE CONCEALED BEHIND ITS AMBIGUOUS AND HUMBLE NAME.

BAR MUT
A bar straight out of a film

And not just because of its New York connection with some of its famous customers, including Woody Allen and Robert de Niro. The founders and proprietors of Bar Mut, Kim Díaz and Eva Pahissa, were working in advertising and film production, when, in 2005, they decided to change the course of their lives. They bought an old bar (the Bar Lis, 1934) in the art nouveau quarter of Barcelona's Eixample district which they had recently used as a location in one of their film shoots. They decided to give it the look and feel of a traditional bodega but using fine materials such as wood, marble and brass that were in keeping with the elegance of the neighbourhood, while retaining some of the bar's original features such as the tiled floor. The concept enabled them to recreate the spirit of the district's bars of the 1930s and 40s in a warm, light-filled ambiance.

A warm, light-filled corner

With this bar, Kim and Eva want their visitors to have a great time and to create a pleasant and beneficial "game of life". In fact, the name of the bar is actually a play on words: in Catalan, "vermut" and "bar mut" are pronounced exactly the same. The former refers to the aromatic fortified wine as well as the appetizers and drinks people have before a meal, and the latter translates as "silent bar" which is perhaps a reference to the phrase "quiet everybody... action!" which is heard so often in their former profession.

After successfully creating such a wonderful interior, they decided that the produce and service – the two other cornerstones of their business – should be of the same high quality. They surrounded themselves with a team of skilled professionals, in the dining area and in the kitchen: a kitchen where Víctor Lema skilfully prepares the finest fish and seafood from the fish markets in Vilanova and Barcelona, as well as the other raw ingredients he sources from small and select suppliers.

The fried egg carpaccio; mum's croquettes; the Bar Mut tuna; the prawns from Vilanova; the chargrilled octopus; the fillet of beef with foie gras; and the Bar Mut rice are just some of the dishes that will make their mark. And for dessert, the famous Spanish take on pain perdu, *torrija*; the chocolate fondant; and the yogurt ice cream with tomato jam and basil oil. You can accompany them with a small draught Estrella Damm beer or a glass of wine from one of 230 handpicked bottles on the wine list. Quiet everybody...we having tapas!

BAR MUT
Carrer de Pau Claris, 192 ▸ Route **8**

AT BAR MUT, KIM DÍAZ AND EVA PAHISSA WISH THEIR DINERS A GREAT CULINARY EXPERIENCE.

TAKTIKA BERRI
From the frying pan to the bar

You can eat some of the finest and tastiest Sant Sebastian-style canapés – *pintxos* – in Barcelona, a city where this way of eating tapas was almost unheard of until the Fernández-Erdocia family decided to leave San Sebastian and reinvent themselves – economically speaking, of course – in the Catalan capital almost two decades ago.

Their gastronomic credentials, consistent with the excellent Basque tradition, leave no room for doubt about the authenticity and quality of their *pintxos*. Julián Fernández learned to cook at one of the foremost gastronomic associations in San Sebastián – Amaikak-bat and Gaztelubide – and is still a member. His mother, Alejandra Mendiburu, discovered the best-kept secrets of Basque cuisine in the kitchen of the farmhouse where she grew up. Julián's wife, Carmen Erdocia, who is the brains behind the success of Taktika Berri, has had the good fortune to have them both as her teachers.

A traditional Basque-style display board welcomes us at the door of Taktika

Every day, Julián and Carmen, together with their daughter María, who is head waitress, offer their loyal diners their famous hot and cold *pintxos*, freshly made with love, know-how and top-quality produce. Their clients come back time and time again because of the welcome they receive and the quality of the food which hasn't diminished with their success. If you are a "berri" ("newcomer" in Basque) at the Taktika, you'll have to keep a close eye on the continuous parade of trays of *pintxos* coming straight out of the kitchen to the bar to make sure you don't miss some of the classics: the *ensaladillas* (potato salads with added tuna or piquillo peppers); *gildas* (green chilli pepper, olive and anchovy served on a cocktail stick); the *tortillas* (potato or salt cod omelettes); the *zamburiñas* (variegated scallops); the *morcilla de Sotopalacios* (blood sausage from Burgos); the croquettes; the *chistorra de Vera de Bidasoa* (a thin cured sausage); and the fish dishes, including the battered cod and hake, which are some of the best you'll find in Barcelona. And, of course, you have to leave room for dessert, such as the cream and wild strawberry millefeuille, the cheese crème caramel and the *coca de Llavaneres*, a special sweet flatbread.

And what about the drinks to go with the *pintxos*? Well, if you follow the Basque tradition you have several choices besides the small glasses of beer known as zuritos: the chacolí de Guetaria (Basque white wine), still Asturian cider and, of course, young red Riojas, a classic element of the "txikiteo" (which in Basque means to go from bar to bar to have small glasses of wine known as "txikitos"). *Goza ezazu!* (Enjoy!).

YOU CAN ALSO EAT SOME OF
THE FINEST DONOSTIA-STYLE
CANAPÉS – *PINTXOS* – AND
TAPAS IN BARCELONA.

85

BODEGA 1900
Our daily "vermut"...

Albert Adrià managed to shake off the labels "Ferran Adrià's little brother", "the pastry chef from elBulli" and "the miniBulli" some time ago. The facts speak for themselves: he was named international chef of the year in 2013 by The Daily Meal; his restaurants Tickets and 41° hold one Michelin star apiece; another of his restaurants Pakta won its first Michelin star in 2014; Tickets was named one of the World's 50 Best Restaurants and Albert was also voted the World's Best Pastry Chef in the same ranking.

For Albert, Bodega 1900, which opened at the end of 2013 without much fanfare, offers a fresh approach to creative cuisine and evokes his childhood experiences, when his father would take him to the neighbourhood bodega for the traditional pre-lunch drink and snack, known as a "vermut".

The bar is housed in a building dating from 1900 – hence its name – and Albert was responsible for the interior décor. His aim was to making his customers feel as if they were stepping inside a time-honoured bodega that has been in the neighbourhood for many years.

Albert Adrià was also responsible for the interior décor of Bodega 1900

Albert Adrià at Bodega 1900

And what does a time-honoured "vermut" consist of? Well, vermouth, of course. The Bodega 1900 has 12 varieties, some of them leading international brands and others produced by small local wineries. Among them is a coupage that Martini makes exclusively for Albert. You can also enjoy a refreshing glass of draught Estrella Damm beer or a glass of wine from the carefully chosen wine list. And to follow, just like any traditional bodega, there's salted fish and meat, as well as preserves, pickles, cured meats and sausages, all of them prepared by the bodega, with the exception of the cockles and Joselito cured meats (the premium brand of Iberico hams). They also serve a number of hot dishes cooked on the hob or on charcoal.

To begin the "vermuteo" nothing beats a bowl of home-made crisps with a special sauce *La Cala de Albert Adrià*, some spicy pork scratchings, San Filippo anchovies or stuffed olives (the most elBulli-like creation on the menu). You can follow these with the smoked meat platter, bonito belly with a spicy dressing, the wind-dried tuna with almonds and the razor clams in a white escabeche pickle. If you fancy something hot, you can try the croquettes made from Joselito Iberico ham, the chargrilled foie gras, the spit-roasted poussin, the pluma ibérica pork and one of the stews of the day. And to end with, irresistible desserts (don't forget Albert's moniker "the World's Best Pastry Chef") which always include a fruit option: melon with vermouth; strawberry and cream millefeuille; apricot ice cream torte; carrot cake or chocolate fritters. Bodega 1900: a return to the past on the way to the future.

BODEGA 1900
Carrer de Tamarit, 91 ▶ Route **6**

FOR ALBERT, BODEGA 1900
OFFERS A FRESH APPROACH
TO CREATIVE CUISINE AND
EVOKES HIS CHILDHOOD
EXPERIENCES.

QUIMET & QUIMET
The genuine article since 1914

It all began a century ago when Quimet Pérez's great-grandfather opened this bodega to sell the wines he produced at his vineyards in El Bruc, a town in the county of Anoia. Four generations of Quimets have worked in the bar in the working-class neighbourhood of Poble-sec, just a stone's throw away from the Paral·lel, the avenue which was the Barcelona equivalent of Montmartre in the early 20th century.

Indeed, brother and sister Quimet and Joana Pérez, the great-grandchildren of the first Quimet who run the bar today, lived on the premises and grew up among the barrels and casks, bottles and fridges in this neighbourhood bodega where the locals knew they could go for a bottle of lemonade even if it was midnight. Today, Quimet & Quimet is one of the most charming bars in Barcelona and resembles a museum of wines and spirits. This tiny bar – it has a floor space of 25 m², just three tables and no seating – immediately captivates anyone who stops off here.

25 m² with centuries-old charm and tradition

Quimet Pérez behind the bar of his "museum" of wines, spirits and tapas

The shelves around the bar are lined with bottles of wine, cava, spirits, beers, tins of gourmet foods and posters advertising historic brands. Its excellent selection of drinks – more than 500 varieties that include red vermouth on tap and their own craft beer – is accompanied by an amazing selection of food. Quimet & Quimet doesn't have a kitchen and only serves cold dishes. Far from being a limitation, this has become its trademark and most original feature.

The team at Quimet & Quimet opens the tinned produce in front of its customers and serves them with their own subtle sauce or dressing. The waiters will tell you about tinned foods with a long pedigree and all kinds of superb cheeses, cured sausages and meats and prepare carefully crafted gourmet canapés to order.

Let Quimet and his team advise you on the right combination of tapas and drinks. Although it may be difficult to choose what to try, you mustn't miss the variegated scallops in brine, the garnished tuna belly, the salmon, yoghurt and truffle honey canapé, the thick-cut potato crisps, the asparagus with cane honey and salmon, the mussel and caviar canapé with confit tomato and the *combinados*: different combinations of seafood, smoked fish and meat.

Although the bar is small and soon fills up, the quality of its tapas is inversely proportional to its size, making it a must for lovers of Barcelona tapas. Quimet & Quimet: it's truly scrumptious!

THE QUALITY OF THE TAPAS AND CANAPÉS AT QUIMET & QUIMET IS INVERSELY PROPORTIONAL TO THE SIZE OF THE BAR.

CASA DE TAPES CAÑOTA
Fun tapas in a creative setting

Fun and creativity are exactly what the Iglesias brothers are committed to in their new gastronomic challenge... as well as the quality of the tapas, of course. This strict requirement has run in the family, ever since their father, who had emigrated from Galicia, founded the famous seafood restaurant Rías de Galicia in the 1950s. This commitment to quality has been strengthened by their partnership with the Adrià brothers at Tickets and 41°, which have recently earned one Michelin star apiece.

At the end of 2011, Juan Carlos, Borja and Pedro decided to take the plunge with a completely new and different approach to tapas in Barcelona, in terms of the graphics and concept of the premises.

The new graphics which reflect the relaxed, uninhibited world of Barcelona's comic strips, can be seen throughout Cañota, from the large windows and posters on the outside, to the tableware, the waiters' T-shirts and aprons and the menus (a witty 16-page comic), which are sold as souvenirs.

The world of the comic strip can be seen throughout Cañota

Juan Carlos and Borja Iglesias inside their bar

The new concept has been made even more enjoyable with the introduction of *foodgets*, such as Little Red Riding Hood's basket and Russian Roulette. These are often accompanied by little performances when they are served. Cañota has also introduced "taparets" (a new word combining tapas and cabaret) and other events featuring actors.

And you can still find what's essential here: excellent, time-honoured tapas created under the supervision of head chef Liberio, and with the collaboration of a guest "star chef" who makes his mark on the menu. Dani García, Paco Roncero – both with two Michelin stars – and Arzak – who holds three – have been invited so far.

Juan Carlos Iglesias personally recommends the Cañota sangria or a refreshing glass of Estrella Damm beer to accompany the top ten dishes of the house: *patatas bravas* made with baked Galician potatoes served with Albert Adrià's sauce; Iberico ham croquettes; *pulpo a feira* (sliced octopus sprinkled with paprika and served on a wooden board); Dani García's burguerbull; the fried fish and seafood box with a pilpil dipping sauce; El Romero Iberico ham from Salamanca; cubes of PGI suckling pig; Russian salad with salmon roe; Lolín 00 anchovies with their secret sauce; and the prawns from Palamós. And we mustn't forget the sweet tapas. Now it's time to dunk your spoon: *cocorrón* pineapple (with a surprise); *crema catalana* with mango; Paco Roig's chocolate ingot; and, of course, Russian Roulette (eight chocolates by Escribà, one of them very, very "explosive"). Dare you play?

CAÑOTA IS COMMITTED TO A NEW CONCEPT OF CULINARY FUN IN A CREATIVE ENVIRONMENT AS WELL AS THE QUALITY OF ITS TAPAS.

TAPAS
Barcelona

40
Recipes

FRIED ARTICHOKES

25 min | serves 4

2 artichokes / 50 g plain flour / 50 g cornflour / 200 ml olive oil / 1 lemon / salt

1 Remove the tough outer leaves of the artichokes, trim the stalk and tips, leaving just the heart. Scrape out the furry choke with a teaspoon. Finely slice the artichokes (or you can use a mandoline) and immerse in a bowl of water with the lemon juice.

2 Heat the oil. Combine the two types of flour with a pinch of salt. Drain the artichoke slices and pat dry with kitchen paper or a clean cloth and dip into the flour. Shake off any excess flour.

3 Place the artichokes into the hot oil and fry until golden. Remove with a slotted spoon and leave to drain on kitchen paper. Repeat with the remainder of the artichokes and serve while hot.

ROASTED VEGETABLE SALAD

50 min | serves 4

1 red bell pepper / 1 aubergine / 1 onion / ½ garlic clove / 8 anchovies / 8 slices of bread / 4 spoonfuls extra virgin olive oil / salt

1 Wash the pepper and aubergine and place on a baking tray together with the whole onion. Bake in a pre-heated oven at 200 °C for 35-40 minutes until the vegetables are tender. The vegetables can be barbecued instead to add extra flavour.

2 Leave the vegetables to cool, peel them and remove the seeds from the pepper. Cut them into strips, lightly salt and keep to one side on a plate.

3 Toast the bread and rub with a little garlic. Place the vegetables and anchovies on top and drizzle with olive oil.

TOMATO, SPRING ONION AND TUNA BELLY SALAD

15 min | serves 4

2 tomatoes / 1 spring onion / 150 g tinned tuna belly in olive oil / 4 spoonfuls extra virgin olive oil / 12 arbequina olives / salt / pepper

1 Clean the onion, slice and leave to soak in water, vinegar and salt for 15 minutes. Clean and hull the tomatoes and cut into segments.

2 Open the tin of tuna and drain. Place the tomato and drained onion on small plates and scatter the tuna belly on top. Lightly season with salt and pepper, a glug of olive oil and sprinkle the olives on top.

3 Serve with finely sliced crunchy flat-bread (if you can't find the typical pan de coca you can use ciabatta instead).

CATALAN-STYLE BROAD BEANS

35 min | serves 4

600 g tender broad beans / 2 spring onions / 2 potatoes / 2 sprigs of mint / 100 g catalan black sausage (botifarra negra) or any kind of blood sausage / 1 glass white wine (optional) / 4 spoonfuls olive oil / salt / pepper

1 Peel the potatoes and cut into small chunks. Clean the onions and cut in half, then in slices lengthwise. Slice the sausage.

2 Heat the oil in a casserole dish and fry the sausage until crisp. Remove and put to one side. In the same oil, sauté the onions for one minute. Add the potatoes, broad beans and a sprig of mint. Add the wine and a small glass of water. Season with salt and pepper, cover and leave to cook on a low heat for 15 minutes.

3 Remove the lid and add the sausage, stir gently and leave for 3-4 minutes to allow the water to evaporate. Adjust the seasoning and remove the mint sprig. Add the rest of the fresh mint leaves and serve immediately.

PORCINI MUSHROOM CROQUETTES

45 min + resting time | for 30 croquettes

300 g porcini mushrooms / 1 onion / 2 tablespoons olive oil / 40 g butter / 3 large spoonfuls flour (60 g) / ¾ litre milk / 2 eggs / 150 g breadcrumbs / 300 ml oil for frying

1 Clean the mushrooms by peeling the stalks, wash quickly and finely dice. Peel the onion and finely dice.

2 Heat the oil and butter and fry the onion for 3-4 minutes. Add the mushrooms and cook for a further 4-5 minutes. Add the flour and lightly brown. Slowly add all the milk, stirring constantly and continue to cook on a low flame for 6-7 minutes, stirring occasionally until the mixture thickens into a paste. Turn into a bowl and leave to cool completely (2-3 hours at least).

3 Once the paste has thickened further, shape into croquettes using two spoons and dip in breadcrumbs, followed by beaten egg and then again in the breadcrumbs, making sure they are evenly coated.

4 Heat the oil and fry the croquettes on all sides until golden. Remove and leave to drain on absorbent kitchen paper.

RUSSIAN SALAD

30 min | serves 4

200 g potatoes / 150 g carrots / 100 g green beans / 2 eggs / 160 g tinned tuna in olive oil
For the mayonnaise: 1 egg / 150 ml olive oil / ½ garlic clove / a few drops of lemon juice / salt

1 Peel the potatoes and carrots and dice into 1 cm cubes. Trim the beans and cut into fine strips. Boil the vegetables for 10-12 minutes in plenty of salted water. Drain and rinse under a cold tap.

2 Put the eggs in a pan with water and bring to the boil. Boil for 10 minutes. Drain, immerse in cold water and peel.

3 Make the mayonnaise by putting the raw egg, garlic, oil, a pinch of salt and a few drops of lemon juice into the beaker of a hand-held blender or mixing bowl. Blend to form a smooth emulsion making sure the blender doesn't move.

4 Mix the chopped hard-boiled eggs with the drained tuna and vegetables and combine with the mayonnaise. Place in a serving dish, cover with cling film and keep in the fridge until ready to serve.

POTATO AND ONION OMELETTE

35 min | serves 4

4 eggs / 3 potatoes (650 g) / 1 large onion (200 g) / 150 ml olive oil / salt

1 Peel and slice the potatoes. Peel and slice the onions into fine strips.

2 Heat the oil in a frying pan and fry the onion for a couple of minutes. Add the potato and cook on a medium heat for 15-20 minutes until the potato is tender and slightly golden. Remove with a slotted spoon and drain.

3 Break the eggs into a bowl, beat and add the potato and onion and ½ teaspoon of salt. Heat a spoonful of oil in a 20 cm diameter non-stick frying pan and pour in the egg and potato mixture. Lower the heat and cook the omelette for 2 minutes. Flip it over using a plate, return it to the pan and cook for a further 2 minutes.

4 Remove, leave to cool slightly and serve with bread rubbed with tomato, a pinch of salt and a drizzle of olive oil.

FRIED POTATO CHUNKS WITH A SPICY TOMATO SAUCE

30 min | serves 4

600 g potatoes / 150 ml olive oil
For the sauce: 200 g puréed tomatoes / 1 or 2 red chillies / 1 egg / 1 garlic clove / 100 ml olive oil /
salt / pepper

1 For the sauce: heat a spoonful of oil in a frying pan, add the tomato and the chillies, salt and pepper and cook with the lid on for 15 minutes.

2 Put the peeled garlic, egg, oil and a pinch of salt into the beaker of a hand-held blender or mixing bowl, and blitz without moving the blender until you have obtained a smooth paste.

3 Peel the potatoes and dice into chunks. Cook in boiling water for 10 minutes and drain.

4 Heat the rest of the oil to 180 °C and fry the potatoes for 3-4 minutes until golden. Drain on kitchen paper and serve on small plates. Top with the tomato sauce and garlic mayonnaise to taste. Serve immediately.

BLACK RICE

40 min | serves 4

300 g round-grain rice / 200 g baby squid / 1 medium-sized cuttlefish with ink / 1 onion / 2 spoonfuls tomato sauce / 1 glass dry white wine / 1 garlic clove / 2 bay leaves / 1.2 litres fish stock / 2 sprigs flat-leaf parsley chopped / 4 spoonfuls olive oil / 1 pot garlic mayonnaise (optional) / salt / pepper

1 Peel the garlic and onion and chop finely. Heat half the oil in a frying pan and sauté the garlic for a few seconds. Add the cleaned, chopped squid, cuttlefish and the ink from both. If using frozen ink, dilute with a spoonful of lukewarm white wine. Sauté for a few seconds, stirring occasionally so they brown evenly.

2 Place a paella pan or large frying pan on the heat, add the remaining oil and fry the onion for 3-4 minutes. Add the rice and stir continuously until the rice starts to colour. Add the parsley, pepper, salt, wine and the fish stock and leave to reduce on a low heat for 8 minutes.

3 Add the sautéed squid, cuttlefish and ink. Adjust the seasoning and cook for a further 8 minutes until the rice is cooked through. To make the dish look more attractive shape with a metal food ring before serving. Serve with garlic mayonnaise if desired.

Blend some parsley leaves with olive oil to make a bright-green oil. It can be used to decorate the finished dish.

SALT COD FRITTERS

45 min | serves 4

150 g shredded salt cod / 250 ml milk / 100 g butter / 150 g flour / 4 eggs / 2 garlic cloves / 2 spoonfuls chopped parsley / salt

1 Rinse the cod thoroughly, finely shred, rinse again and leave to soak for 1 hour, changing the water every so often.

2 Meanwhile, heat the milk, butter and a pinch of salt. Once it starts to boil, reduce the heat, add the flour in one go and stir vigorously with a wooden spoon.

3 When the paste has thickened and begins to stick to the sides of the pan, remove from the heat and stir for a few minutes to allow it cool.

4 Once cooled slightly, add the eggs one by one, beating with a whisk (an electric whisk is preferable) making sure that each one is blended before you add the next.

5 Add the chopped garlic and the cod, first checking that it isn't too salty. Blend well, add the parsley and mix together. Place balls of the mixture into hot oil and allow them to puff up. Remove the fritters once golden, drain on kitchen paper and serve hot.

The oil should be moderately hot. If it is too hot, the fritters may be raw in the middle even though they are golden brown on the outside. Test the first batch and reduce the temperature of the oil accordingly.

FRIED WHITEBAIT

20 min | serves 4

600 g fresh anchovies / 1 egg / 1 cup flour for frying / 1 cup oil for frying / salt

1 Remove the heads and innards of the anchovies and rinse carefully under running water. Drain and dry on kitchen paper.

2 Beat and season the egg. Dip the fish in the egg and flour and fry in hot oil for a couple of minutes. Remove and leave to drain on kitchen paper.

3 Season and serve straight away with a tomato and olive salad if desired.

Even though it's more expensive, it's better to fry the fish in olive oil. It's tastier and healthier too!

The fish can be fried without the egg making it lighter, but just as delicious.

CHARGRILLED SARDINES WITH GARLIC AND PARSLEY

15 min | serves 4

12 medium-sized sardines / 1 garlic clove / 1 small bunch of parsley / olive oil / coarse salt / salt

1 Sprinkle the sardines generously with coarse salt and leave to stand for at least 30 minutes. Then rinse them under running water and remove the innards. Descale the sardines only if the scales are thick.

2 Peel and chop the garlic. Wash the parsley, dry with kitchen paper and finely chop.

3 Grill the sardines over embers, on a hot plate or in a griddle pan with a few drops of olive oil for 2 minutes on each side.

4 Season with a pinch of salt and add the chopped garlic and parsley. Grill for a further 30 seconds and remove from the heat. Serve immediately.

If the sardines are very fresh, there's no need to gut them. They won't need descaling if they are to be cooked on a barbecue unless the scales are very thick. Sardine scales can be removed very easily by rubbing a finger or a sheet of kitchen paper over the fish.

BATTERED SQUID RINGS

20 min | serves 4

2 medium-sized squid / 200 g flour / 1 lemon / 2 eggs / olive oil / salt

1 Clean the squid by removing the in-nards, quill and beak. Chop up the tentacles and cut the body into 1cm-thick rings.

2 Juice the lemon and sprinkle over the squid. Leave to marinate for at least 30 minutes. Meanwhile, beat the eggs in a dish and put the flour in another.

3 Dip the squid in the flour followed by the egg. Fry in batches in a frying pan with plenty of hot oil.

4 Leave to drain on kitchen paper, season and serve immediately.

Serve with lemon wedges if desired.

MACKEREL IN AN ESCABECHE PICKLE

50 min + resting time | serves 4

2 medium-sized mackerel / 1 carrot / 1 onion / 3 glasses white wine / 1 glass sherry vinegar /
2 cloves garlic / 1 bay leaf / 1 small bunch of parsley / 4 black peppercorns / salt

1 Peel and slice the carrot and onion. Peel and finely slice the garlic. Clean the mackerel, remove the guts and heads and cut into 4 cm-wide slices.

2 To make the escabeche, place the white wine and vinegar in a small casserole dish with the carrot, onion garlic, peppercorns, bay leaf and parsley. Bring to the boil, cover and cook on a low heat for 30 minutes.

3 Place the mackerel in a flat dish and cover completely with the escabeche.

4 Cover the dish and cook on a low heat for 8 minutes. Take off the heat and leave to cool in the liquid. Once cool, place in the fridge for at least 12 hours to absorb the flavours.

5 Remove from the fridge and serve at room temperature.

Escabeche is a traditional Spanish pickling method used to preserve foods. For the best results, keep the pickled fish in the fridge for two to three days. The same recipe can be used with other oily fish (tuna, sardines, horse mackerel...) as well as quail or chicken.

BATTERED MONKFISH AND ARTICHOKE SKEWERS

15 min | serves 4

300 g monkfish loin / 2 medium-sized artichokes / 1 lemon / 1 egg / 4 spoonfuls flour / olive oil / pepper / salt

1   Cut the monkfish loin into 2 cm chunks.

2   Prepare the artichokes by removing ⅔ of the tip, the stems and outer leaves. Cut into quarters and remove the choke. Rub with lemon to prevent them discolouring.

3   Thread a small skewer alternating two chunks of monkfish with two of artichoke. Do the same with the remaining three skewers.

4   Dip the skewers into the flour followed by the beaten egg and fry in a large frying pan with plenty of hot olive oil.

5   Place on kitchen paper to drain off the excess oil, season with salt and pepper and serve immediately.

The skewers can be served with a dipping sauce: soy sauce, teriyaki sauce, romesco...

CATALAN-STYLE SALT COD

30 min | serves 4

4 salt cod loins previously soaked to remove the salt / 1 tomato / 2 garlic cloves
1 teaspoon paprika / 1 glass white wine / olive oil / pepper / salt / parsley

1 Pat the cod loins dry with kitchen paper and dust with flour. Fry for one minute on each side in a frying pan with two spoonfuls of hot olive oil. Drain again on kitchen paper and place in an ovenproof dish.

2 Fry the chopped garlic in the same oil until lightly golden – do not let it brown too much or it will taste bitter. Add grated tomato, season with salt and pepper and a pinch of paprika. Cook for 5 minutes before adding the white wine. Increase the heat and reduce the sauce for two minutes.

3 Pour the sauce over the cod and bake in a preheated oven at 200 °C for 8 minutes. Sprinkle with chopped parsley and serve immediately.

The dish is called *"bacallà a la llauna"* in Catalan. The name *"llauna"* ("tin" in Catalan) refers to the dish or metal tray the fish is baked in.

RAW COD SALAD

15 minutes + resting time | serves 4

300 g cod loin / 1 large tomato / 1 small onion / ½ green bell pepper / ½ red bell pepper /
12 black olives / olive oil / pepper

1 Rinse the cod under running water and tear into irregular strips. Leave the strips to soak in water for 4-5 hours.

2 Peel and finely slice the onions. Wash, dry and grate the tomato. Wash and dry the peppers and chop into chunks.

3 Place the grated tomato on a serving plate. Drain the cod and place on top of the tomato. Add the sliced onions, the pepper chunks and black olives. Season with a pinch of pepper, drizzle over olive oil and keep refrigerated until ready to serve.

The word "esqueixar" means to shred in Catalan. The experts say that for this dish, the cod should not be cut with a knife, but simply torn with the fingers.

RED MULLET WITH TOMATO AND CAPER SALSA

30 min | serves 4

8 medium-sized red mullet / 2 tomatoes / 1 spring onion / 3 spoonfuls capers in vinegar / 1 lemon / 1 garlic clove / 4 spoonfuls olive oil / 2 bunches parsley / 1 glass white wine / 1 pinch hot paprika / salt / pepper

1 Peel the garlic and onion and chop. Wash the tomatoes and dice. Mix in a bowl with the capers, chopped parsley, salt and pepper and pour over almost all the oil and wine.

2 Clean the red mullet: cut open the belly with scissors, remove the innards and rinse. Dry with kitchen paper and place on an oven tray greased with the remaining oil.

3 Pour the salsa and a squirt of lemon over the fish. Place in a preheated oven at 180 °C for 12-15 minutes depending on the size of the red mullet. Serve immediately with just-cooked fresh pasta if desired.

Drizzling the fish with lemon juice before placing in the oven will give it a fresh Mediterranean taste.

TUNA CUBE WITH TOMATO CONFIT

40 min | serves 4

4 cubes tuna belly (50 g each) / 2 tomatoes / 20 g brown sugar / 1 spoonful soya sauce / chives / pepper / coarse salt flakes

1 Cut a cross in the base of the tomatoes and scald in a pan of boiling water for 2 minutes. Drain and cool under running water. Peel them, remove the seeds and chop.

2 Put the prepared tomato in a frying pan or heavy-based pan with the sugar and three spoonfuls of water. Cook on a low heat for 20 minutes, stirring regularly.

The cooking time of the tuna is a matter of individual taste. It can also be prepared like tataki by flash frying and then submerging it in a bowl of water and ice to stop it cooking further.

3 Flash fry the tuna cubes with a few drops of olive oil on a griddle or in a non-stick frying pan for 30 seconds on each side.

4 Serve the hot tuna cubes on a small plate or a Chinese soup spoon on a bed of warm tomato confit. Season with a few drops of soy sauce, salt flakes, freshly ground pepper and some chopped chives.

TELLIN CLAMS WITH GARLIC AND PARSLEY

10 min | serves 4

300 g tellin clams (coquina or any small clams) / 2 garlic cloves / 1 bunch of parsley /
2 spoonfuls of olive oil

1 Leave the clams to soak in salted water for a few hours to get rid of any sand or grit.

2 Peel and chop the garlic cloves. Wash the parsley under running water, dry with kitchen paper and finely chop.

3 Heat two spoonfuls of olive oil in a non-stick frying pan and gently fry the garlic without allowing it to colour.

4 Add the clams and stir for a few seconds until they open. Sprinkle with parsley and serve immediately.

A squeeze of lemon can be added at the last minute if desired.

Tellin or coquina clams are small bivalve molluscs that are popular throughout the Mediterranean and the north of Spain. Galicia, Huelva and Cadiz are the main centres of production as well as some sandy areas along the Mediterranean coast.

GRIDDLED RAZOR CLAMS WITH LEMON OIL

10 min | serves 4

16 razor clams / 1 garlic clove / 1 bunch parsley / olive oil
For the lemon oil: 1 cup olive oil / ½ cup lemon juice

1 Lemon oil: combine the olive oil with the lemon juice, stir and leave to stand for at least 6 hours to absorb the flavour.

2 Rinse the razor clams and leave in salted water for 30 minutes to get rid of any sand or grit. Peel and chop the garlic. Wash the parsley, dry with kitchen paper and finely chop.

3 Heat some drops of olive oil in a griddle pan or non-stick frying pan and sauté the razor clams until they open. Sprinkle with the garlic and parsley mix and dress with lemon oil.

4 Sauté for another minute, transfer to a serving dish and serve straight away.

When made in a frying pan, the cooking liquid from the razor clams can be used to make a quick lemon sauce by simply adding a pinch of flour dissolved in water to thicken.

SMALL PRAWNS WITH GARLIC AND PARSLEY

10 min | serves 4

200 g small prawns / 2 garlic cloves / 1 bunch parsley / olive oil / salt

1__Remove the longer whiskers from the prawns. Peel and chop the garlic cloves. Wash the parsley under running water, pat dry with kitchen paper and finely chop.

2__Heat a spoonful of oil and fry the prawns in two batches for one minute on each side. Sprinkle with salt and remove from the pan.

3__Add two more spoonfuls of oil to the same frying pan and sauté the chopped garlic until it starts to colour. Sprinkle with parsley and pour the mixture over the prawns. Serve immediately.

It is preferable to fry the prawns in batches to make it easier to turn them over and allow them to cook more evenly. Cooking time will depend on the size of the prawns.

It is better to fry the prawns in a small amount of oil and, once cooked, to remove them and add more oil to the pan so it takes on the delicious flavour of the remaining juices. It is essential to serve the dish with bread to mop up the sauce!

SPICY MUSSELS WITH TOMATO

35 min | serves 4

400 g mussels / 1 spring onion / 100 ml tomato sauce / 1 small chilli pepper / 4 spoonfuls white wine / 2 garlic cloves / 1 teaspoon brown sugar / 1 bunch parsley / pepper

1 Clean the mussels under running water and remove the beards. Peel and finely chop the onion and garlic. Wash the parsley, pat dry and finely chop.

2 Heat two spoonfuls of oil in a non-stick frying pan and fry the onion on a low heat for 8 minutes. Add the garlic and chilli and sauté for 1 more minute.

3 Add the tomato sauce, a pinch of pepper and the sugar and fry for a further 5 minutes.

4 Cook the mussels with the wine in a covered pan for 4 minutes. Stir with a wooden spoon halfway through the cooking time. Drain the mussels and set aside four spoonfuls of strained cooking liquor.

5 Add the cooking liquor to the tomato sauce and cook for 2 more minutes. Add the mussels, stir and cook for another minute. Adjust the seasoning with a pinch of salt if necessary, sprinkle with plenty of chopped parsley and serve immediately.

It is important to be careful when seasoning the tomato sauce. Once the cooking liquor from the mussels has been added, you don't usually need to add any extra salt.

CLAMS WITH HARICOT BEANS AND WHITE WINE

35 min | serves 4

200 g cooked haricot beans / 150 g clams / ½ green bell pepper / 1 small cup fish stock / 4 spoonfuls white wine / ½ teaspoon flour / ½ onion / 1 garlic clove / olive oil / pepper / salt

1 Leave the clams to soak in salted water for at least 6 hours to release any sand or grit.

2 Peel and chop the onion and the garlic clove. Wash and dry the bell pepper and cut into chunks.

3 Heat two spoonfuls of oil in a non-stick frying pan and sauté the chopped onion for 8 minutes. Add the garlic and bell pepper and fry for another 5 minutes.

4 Add the clams and leave for 2-3 minutes until they open. Add the white wine and increase the heat for a few seconds until all the alcohol evaporates. Dissolve the flour in the fish stock and add to the pan.

5 Add the beans, season with a pinch of pepper, adjust the salt and bring to the boil.

6 Leave to cook on a low heat for a few minutes to allow the sauce to thicken. Sprinkle with plenty of chopped parsley and serve.

The same recipe can be used for cockles. The dish should always have a fairly soupy consistency, but this is a matter of individual taste. This is a delicious winter stew.

POTATO AND LOBSTER SLICE WITH SALSA VERDE

35 min | serves 4

1 large potato / 1 lobster tail / a pinch of smoked paprika / a handful of toasted corn / chives / salt flakes / salt
For the salsa verde: 1 garlic clove / 1 bunch parsley / ½ cup oil / 1 spoonful lemon juice / salt

1 Salsa verde: Put the garlic and oil into the beaker or bowl of a blender. Add the chopped parsley and blend to make a thick bright-green sauce. Add the lemon juice, season with a pinch of salt and put to one side.

2 Cut the potato into 1 cm-thick slices. Heat plenty of oil in a pan without letting it boil and add the potatoes (the temperature should be between 85 °C- 90 °C approximately). Cook the potatoes for 10-12 minutes and drain.

3 Grind the corn to a powder. Cook the lobster tail in a pot with salted water for 6 minutes. Drain, leave to cool and remove the shell. Brush the tail lightly with olive oil, coat in the corn powder and cut into thick slices.

4 Place a slice of potato on a plate, season with a pinch of salt and smoked pa- prika. Place a slice of the lobster coated in the corn powder on top and season with salt flakes. Sprinkle with a pinch of chopped chives. Drizzle with the salsa verde, decorate with some whole chive stems and serve.

This tapa can also be made with cooked octopus. The salsa verde can be substituted with a mango and vanilla vinaigrette.

KING PRAWNS IN TEMPURA BATTER WITH ROMESCO SAUCE AND CURLY ENDIVE

1 h 10 min | serves 4

12 king prawns / 1 cup + 2 spoonfuls flour / 1 egg yolk / 1 cup very cold water / curly endive leaves
For the romesco sauce: 1 tomato / ½ onion / 50 g hazelnuts / 1 choricero or ñora pepper (or any dried sweet red bell peppers) / 1 garlic clove / 100 ml olive oil / 50 ml vinegar / pepper / salt

1 Romesco: Put the onion and tomato in an ovenproof dish with a glug of olive oil and roast at 200 °C for 40 minutes. Halfway through, add the unpeeled garlic clove. Remove from the oven, peel and blend in a food processor with the remaining oil and vinegar, the flesh of the pepper and the hazelnuts with their skins removed. Season with salt and pepper and blend further until you obtain a sauce.

2 Make the tempura by beating the flour with an egg yolk and very cold water (you can add ice cubes).

3 Thread the prawns onto a small skewer and dip into the tempura batter. Fry in batches in a pan with plenty of hot oil and leave to drain on kitchen paper.

4 Divide the curly endive leaves between four bowls or small plates and place the skewers on top. Drizzle with the romesco sauce and serve immediately.

The king prawns can be fried in a more traditional batter made from flour, water or beer, a dash of oil and a pinch of baking powder or, alternatively, 'a la romana', by dipping them in flour followed by beaten egg.

Romesco sauce is a traditional Catalan sauce. It can be bought ready-made from supermarkets in Spain.

OCTOPUS IN A VINAIGRETTE DRESSING

50 minutes + resting time | serves 4

1 medium-sized octopus / ½ spring onion / ¼ red bell pepper / ¼ green bell pepper / 6 gherkins
For the vinaigrette: 6 spoonfuls olive oil / 2 spoonfuls sherry vinegar / pepper / salt

1 Clean the octopus by removing the innards, eyes and the beak. Hold the octopus by the head and dunk it three times in a pan of boiling salted water. Return to the pan and simmer for 35 minutes and leave to cool in the cooking water. Drain and chop with scissors.

2 Wash the peppers and cut into chunks. Peel and dice the onion. Finely dice the gherkins.

3 Prepare the vinaigrette by whisking all the ingredients together to make an emulsion.

4 Place the octopus pieces in a bowl or on a serving plate. Put the diced vegetables on top and dress with the vinaigrette. Keep in the fridge for 3 to 4 hours and serve well chilled.

The octopus is dipped three times in boiling water before cooking so that the skin does not come away during the cooking process. It also helps to freeze, then defrost the octopus beforehand to break down the tissue and tenderise it.

BABY CUTTLEFISH WITH PEAS

45 min | serves 4

4 baby cuttlefish / 100 g peas / 1 spring onion / 1 garlic clove / ½ glass white wine / 1 bunch of parsley / 1 pinch sugar / 1 pinch nutmeg / 1 pinch cinnamon / pepper / salt

1 Clean the cuttlefish by removing the quill, the innards, the eyes and the beak. Heat a spoonful of oil in a wide pan and sauté for 2 minutes on both sides. Season with salt and pepper, remove and put to one side.

2 Add another spoonful of oil to the pan and sauté the diced onion on a low heat for 10 minutes. Add the chopped garlic and cook for another minute.

3 Return the cuttlefish to the pan and add the white wine. Turn up the heat for a few seconds to burn off the alcohol.

4 Add the peas, season with salt and pepper and a pinch of sugar, ground nutmeg and cinnamon. Add a glass of water, cover and continue cooking for 12 minutes. Take the lid off the pan and cook for 2 minutes longer until the liquid has almost reduced completely. Sprinkle with the chopped parsley and serve immediately.

The cooking time should be increased if using larger cuttlefish even if it's cut into pieces. You can also make a 'surf and turf' version of this dish by adding meatballs and a couple of spoonfuls of tomato sauce. This is a popular variant in the Empordà region of the Costa Brava.

MORCILLA ONION SAUSAGE WITH CHICKPEAS

40 min | serves 4

4 small Spanish morcilla onion sausages (or any small blood sausage) / 250 g cooked chickpeas /
1 onion / 1 tomato / ½ green bell pepper / 1 carrot / 1 garlic clove / 1 teaspoon paprika / 1 bunch
of parsley / a glug of brandy / olive oil / pepper / salt

1 Brown the sausages for 30 seconds in a pan with a spoonful of oil. Remove and put to one side.

2 Add another spoonful of oil to the pan and sauté the diced onion on a low heat for 10 minutes. Add the chopped garlic, diced carrot and bell pepper. Cook for a further 2 minutes and add the grated tomato.

3 Add a glug of brandy, season with salt, pepper and the paprika. Leave to cook on a low heat for 10 minutes.

4 Add the sausages, three spoonfuls of stock or water and the cooked chickpeas. Cook for a further 5 minutes making sure that the sausages don't break up. Sprinkle generously with chopped parsley and serve immediately.

The sauce can be thickened using a blend of crushed almonds, parsley and garlic or by adding half a teaspoon of flour dissolved in lukewarm water.

«CAP I POTA»

1 h 10 min + resting time | serves 4

200 g cooked flesh from a cow's head and feet / 100 g cooked cow tripe / 20 g spicy chorizo sausage / 25 g chopped ham / 40 g smoked bacon / 3 tomatoes / 1 green bell pepper / 1 onion / 1 garlic clove / ½ chilli / 1 glass of white wine / 1 teaspoon paprika / 1 bay leaf / pepper / salt

1 Wash the flesh from the head and feet and the tripe and cook in a pan with plenty of salted water and the bay leaf. Bring to the boil and cook on a low heat for 35 minutes. Drain, leave to cool and chop into pieces. Put a few spoonfuls of the cooking liquor to one side.

2 Sauté the diced onion in a pan on a low heat for 10 minutes. Add the chopped ham and smoked bacon and cook for another 5 minutes. Add the chopped garlic, chorizo sausage and bell pepper. Cook for 5 more minutes.

3 Add the grated tomato, season with the salt, pepper and paprika. Pour in the white wine and briefly turn up the heat to reduce. Lower the heat again and cook for 10 minutes.

4 Add the finely chopped flesh from the head and feet and the tripe. Season with salt and pepper again and add the chilli. Add a spoonful of the cooking liquor and cook on a low heat for 40 minutes. Leave to stand for at least 2 hours before serving.

This hearty Catalan dish is often served with the classic vegetable "samfaina" stew (a Catalan version of ratatouille). You can also add chickpeas.

You can buy ready-cooked tripe but even then it is better to repeat the cooking process for 30-35 minutes, although not essential.

CUTTLEFISH WITH MEATBALLS

1 h | serves 4

2 medium-sized cuttlefish / 150 g minced beef / 150 g minced pork / 1 egg / 2 garlic cloves /
2 bunches of parsley / 2 medium onions / 1 slice of rustic-style bread / 1 small cup milk / 1 cup
flour / 3 spoonfuls puréed tomato / 1 glass white wine / 1 cup + 2 spoonfuls olive oil / salt / pepper

1_ Peel and chop the onions and one garlic clove. Heat two spoonfuls of oil in a pan and sauté the onion and garlic for 15 minutes. Add the puréed tomato and continue frying for 10 minutes.

2_ Peel the remaining garlic clove and chop finely. Wash the parsley and remove the leaves and finely chop. Put the meat in a bowl. Add the egg, garlic, parsley and the bread which has been soaked in milk and squeezed out. Season with salt and pepper and mix well by hand. Form into walnut-sized balls and roll in flour.

3_ Heat the remaining oil in a frying pan, fry the meatballs, turning them over until golden on all sides and remove from the heat.

4_ Put them in the pan with the tomato and onion sauce and pour in the wine. Allow to reduce for a few minutes, cover with water and cook on a low heat for 30 minutes, adding more water if required.

Add a picada made from 1 garlic clove, 5 toasted almonds and 1 spoonful of chopped parsley at the end of cooking for a richer flavour.

FRICANDEAU WITH WILD MUSHROOMS

1 h 10 min | serves 4

8 finely sliced topside beef steaks / 1 handful of dried wild mushrooms (Scotch bonnets, fairy rings or chanterelles) / 2 tomatoes / 1 onion / 1 cup stock or water / 1 glass white wine / 1 cup + 1 spoonful flour / 2 spoonfuls olive oil / 1 bay leaf / salt / pepper
For the picada sauce: 1 spoonful toasted almonds / 1 garlic clove / 1 spoonful chopped parsley

1 Soak the mushrooms in lukewarm water for 20 minutes. Season the steaks, dip in flour and fry in a pan with a spoonful of hot oil. Remove from the pan.

2 Fry the chopped onion in the same oil on a low heat for 15 minutes. Add the chopped tomatoes and continue to cook for 10 minutes. Add a spoonful of flour, stir and cook for 2 minutes.

The dried Scotch bonnets, fairy rings or chanterelles add a very special flavour to the tomato sauce. Add the water from the soaked tomatoes instead of the stock for additional flavour.

3 Pour in the white wine and add the drained mushrooms and bay leaf. Leave to cook for 2 minutes before adding the stock. Season and continue cooking on a low heat for 10 minutes. Add the steaks and leave it all to cook for 30 minutes.

4 Pound the toasted almonds, garlic clove and some parsley leaves using a pestle and mortar. Add the picada to the pan and cook for a further 10 minutes. Serve hot.

GIANT SPICY POTATO CROQUETTES

55 min | serves 4

500 g potatoes / 150 g minced beef / 100 ml tomato sauce / 10 drops Tabasco® / 1 onion / 1 garlic clove / 1 cup flour / 1 cup breadcrumbs / 2 eggs / olive oil / pepper / salt

1 Cook the potatoes in their skins in a pan of boiling, salted water for 35 minutes. Drain and leave to cool. Peel and mash with a fork until no lumps remain. Season, add a drizzle of olive oil and mix.

2 Peel and chop the onion and garlic. Fry the onion on a low heat in a frying pan with three spoonfuls of oil for 10 minutes. Add the garlic and fry for 2 more minutes. Add the meat, stir and season with the salt and pepper. Continue cooking for 8 minutes until the meat is cooked through. Add the tomato sauce, season with salt and pepper and the Tabasco®. Cook for another 5 minutes.

3 Take a little of the mashed potato mix and, with damp hands, form it into balls the size of a medium satsuma. Flatten the potato ball and place a spoonful of the meat filling on top. Close the potato over it and reshape into a ball.

4 Roll the croquettes in flour, beaten egg and breadcrumbs and fry in batches in a frying pan with plenty of hot oil. Drain on kitchen paper to get rid of any excess oil and serve immediately.

The traditional filling for these spicy croquettes is minced meat. However, it can be replaced with other ingredients such as tuna, prawns, mushrooms, cheese or spinach according to the chef's taste and imagination.

They can be served with romesco, mayonnaise or spicy tomato sauce.

HAM WITH TOMATO-RUBBED BREAD

5 min | serves 4

150 g serrano ham / 1 crunchy flatbread or ciabatta / 2 ripe juicy tomatoes / 4 spoonfuls extra virgin olive oil / salt

1 Cut the bread in half lengthways and toast. Cut the tomatoes in half and rub on the cut side of the bread.

2 Season with a pinch of salt and plenty of olive oil and cut into portions.

3 Put the ham on top and serve quickly so the bread remains crispy.

MANDARIN SORBET

30 min + freezing time | 4 sorbets

1 kg mandarins (500 ml of juice) / 150 g sugar / 80 ml mineral water / 1 lemon / 2 egg whites

1 Wash and dry 3 mandarins and remove the zest with a grater. Cut them all in half and juice them. Pour the mineral water into a saucepan, add the sugar, bring to the boil and simmer for a couple of minutes. Leave the syrup to cool.

2 Combine the mandarin juice with the zest and the syrup.

3 Put the egg whites into a large mixing bowl and beat with an electric or hand whisk until they form soft peaks. Gradually pour the liquid into the egg whites, carefully stirring and put into the ice-cream maker. If you don't have an ice-cream maker, pour the mixture into a large, metal container and put in the freezer. Stir the mixture every 20 minutes, breaking down the crystals with a fork until the sorbet takes on a smooth and creamy consistency. Whisk again to make the mixture even smoother and return to the freezer.

4 Using an ice-cream scoop, serve the mandarin sorbet in small bowls or sundae dishes.

This refreshing sorbet is perfect for the end of a heavy meal. It can also be served as a palate cleanser between fish and meat dishes

CREMA CATALANA

20 min + resting time | serves 4

½ litre milk / 4 egg yolks / 100 g + 3 spoonfuls sugar / 25 g corn starch / 1 cinnamon stick / 1 piece lemon peel

1 Bring the milk to a boil with the cinnamon and lemon peel. Beat the egg yolks, the sugar (100 g) and corn starch with a whisk and pour in the strained milk. Stir, return to the saucepan and warm over a low heat, stirring continuously until it thickens.

Vanilla and orange makes a delicious substitute for the cinnamon and lemon!

2 Divide the custard into four individual dishes and leave to cool completely in the fridge.

3 Before serving, sprinkle an even layer of sugar on top and caramelize with a branding iron (a metal disc heated on a flame) or a small blow torch.

LENT FRITTERS WITH ALMOND AND ORANGE

45 min | serves 6-8

¼ litre water / 2 spoonfuls sugar / 75 g butter / 150 g flour / 4 eggs / 50 g crushed toasted almonds / zest of half an orange / ½ teaspoon salt / 200 g sugar for dusting / 1 cup olive oil

1 Bring a saucepan containing the water, butter, 2 spoonfuls sugar and salt to the boil. Once it comes to the boil, take off the heat, add the flour in one go and stir vigorously until it forms a sticky ball.

2 Add the eggs one at a time, stirring continuously until each one is incorporated into the mixture. Finally add the almonds and the orange zest and stir well.

3 Form into balls using two teaspoons and drop into the hot oil. Fry for 2-3 minutes on each side until golden, remove with a slotted spoon and drain on kitchen paper. Repeat the process until all the mixture has been used up.

4 Put the sugar into a deep bowl and dredge the fritters while they are still hot.

CONFECTIONER'S CUSTARD AND RASPBERRY MILLEFEUILLE

40 min | serves 6-8

1 sheet puff pastry / 200 g raspberries / 2 spoonfuls icing sugar
For the confectioner's custard: 250 ml milk / 1 cinnamon stick / 1 piece lemon peel / 3 egg yolks /
50 g sugar / 25 g cornflour

1 Pour the milk into a saucepan with the cinnamon stick and lemon peel and bring to the boil. Beat together the three egg yolks and the sugar and add the cornflour. Take the milk off the heat, remove the cinnamon stick and lemon peel and gradually pour over the egg yolks while whisking. Pour into a saucepan and cook on a low heat, stirring continuously until it thickens. Take off the heat and leave to cool completely, giving it an occasional stir.

2 Roll the puff pastry out into a fine layer and cut into 12 equal rectangles. Place them on a baking tray, prick all over with a fork and bake in a preheated oven for 15-20 minutes at 220 °C until golden. Remove from the oven and allow to cool.

3 In the meantime, wash the raspberries and dry well on kitchen paper. Spread the pastry slices with a thin layer of the custard and place one on top of another to make three layers. Place the raspberries on top and sprinkle with icing sugar.

BREAD WITH CHOCOLATE AND EXTRA VIRGIN OLIVE OIL

20 min + resting time | serves 8

3 egg yolks / 200 ml whipping cream / 30 g sugar / 125 g 70% cocoa chocolate / ½ loaf of bread /
6 spoonfuls extra virgin olive oil / 1 teaspoon salt flakes

1 Pour the cream into a saucepan and bring to the boil. Beat the yolks with sugar and add the cream. Stir and return it to the saucepan to cook on a low heat for a couple of minutes stirring continuously.

2 Remove from the heat, add the broken chocolate and stir until melted. Pour into a container. Leave to cool and keep in the fridge for at least a couple of hours.

3 Slice the bread finely, place on an oven tray and brush with some of the olive oil. Toast under the oven grill for 3-4 minutes and remove.

4 When ready to serve the dessert, use a hot spoon to form quenelles (small elongated balls) with the chocolate mixture and place on plates leaving some space between them. Place a piece of toast behind each quenelle and finish off by decorating the plate with some salt flakes and a few drops of olive oil.

CURD CHEESE WITH JAM OR HONEY

5 min | serves 4

4 slices of fresh curd cheese / 4 spoonfuls honey / 30 g pine nuts

1 Spread the pine nuts out on an oven tray and bake in a preheated oven at 200 °C for 5-6 minutes. They can also be toasted in a frying pan without adding anything and stirring occasionally.

2 Divide the curd cheese between the plates. Drizzle over a generous spoonful of honey and finish off with the pine nuts.

It is also traditional to serve the cheese with other dried fruit and nuts such as walnuts, hazelnuts, and raisins.

TAPAS
Barcelona

10
Routes

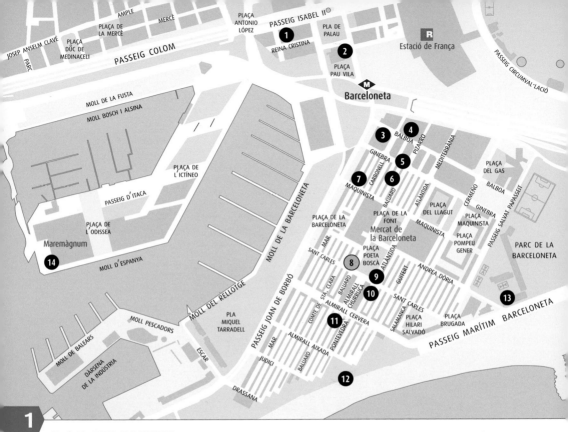

BARCELONETA

BORN

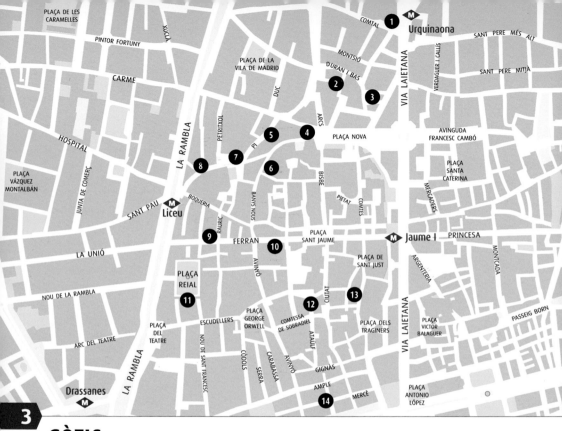

GÒTIC

1 **La Plassohla** Via Laietana, 49

2 **Bosco Food & Drinks** Carrer dels Capellans, 9

3 **La Cala del Vermut** Carrer d'en Copons, 2

4 **Bilbao Berria** Plaça Nova, 3

5 **La Pineda** Carrer del Pi, 16

6 **El Portalón** Carrer dels Banys Nous, 20

7 **Bar del Pi** Plaça de Sant Josep Oriol, 1

8 **Irati Taberna Basca** Carrer del Cardenal Casañas, 17

9 **Adagio Tapas** Carrer de Ferran, 21

10 **Orio BCN Gòtic** Carrer de Ferran, 38

11 **Ocaña** Plaça Reial, 13-15

12 **Bar Mingus** Carrer d'Ataülf, 6

13 **Bodega La Palma** Carrer de la Palma de Sant Just, 7

14 **Bar la Plata** Carrer de la Mercè, 28

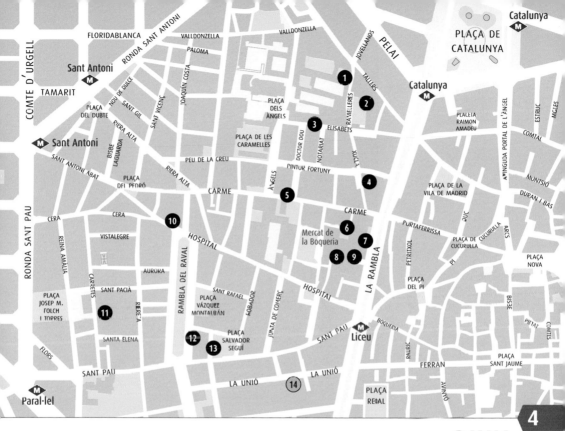

1 **Cèntric Canalla** Carrer de les Ramelleres, 27

2 **Kasparo** Plaça de Vicenç Martorell, 4

3 **Dos Palillos** Carrer d'Elisabets, 9

4 **Bar Lobo** Carrer del Pintor Fortuny, 3

5 **Carmelitas Tapas** Carrer del Carme, 42

6 **Bar Papitu** Passatge de la Virreina, 1

7 **Casa Guinart** La Rambla, 95

8 **Pinotxo** La Rambla, 91 (Mercat Boqueria)

9 **El Quim de la Boqueria** La Rambla, 91 (Mercat Boqueria)

10 **Barraval** Carrer de l'Hospital, 104

11 **Maki Navaja Bar** Carrer de les Carretes, 51

12 **La Taverna del Suculent** Rambla del Raval, 39

13 **La Monroe** Plaça de Salvador Seguí, 1-9

▶ 14 **Cañete** Carrer de la Unió, 17 (p. 18)

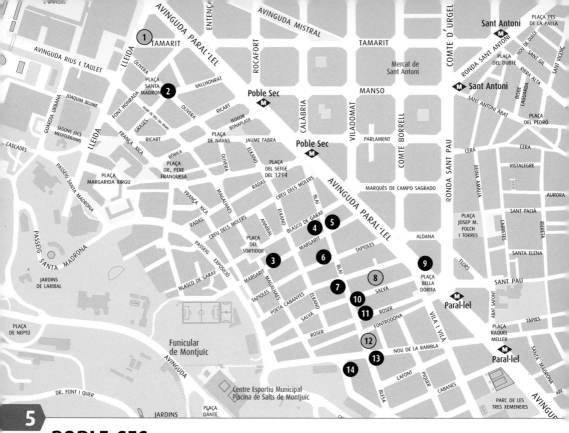

POBLE-SEC

SANT ANTONI

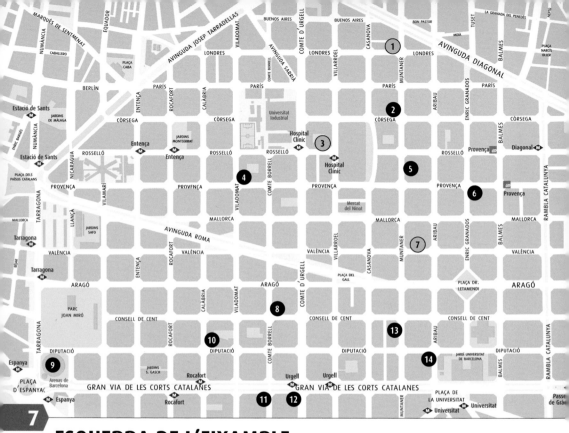

ESQUERRA DE L'EIXAMPLE

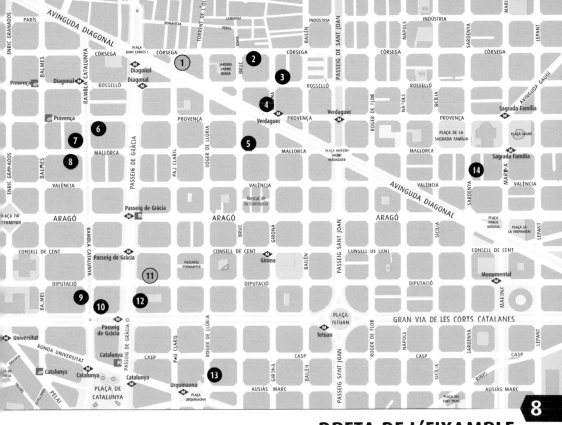

DRETA DE L'EIXAMPLE

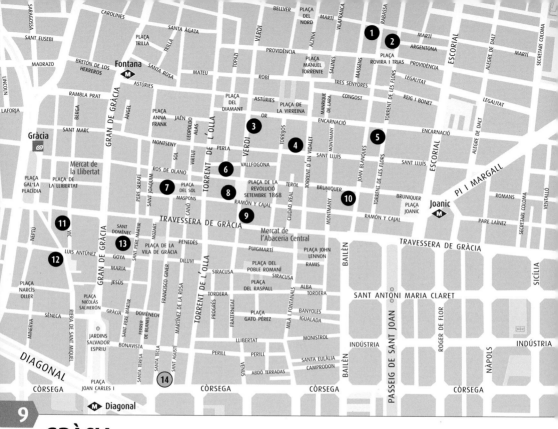

GRÀCIA

1 **Gata Mala** Carrer de Rabassa, 37

2 **Bodega Manolo** Carrer del Torrent de les Flors, 101

3 **D. O.** Carrer de Verdi, 36

4 **Polleria Fontana** Carrer de Sant Lluís, 9

5 **Lata-Berna** Carrer del Torrent de les Flors, 53

6 **La Viblioteca** Carrer de Vallfogona, 12

7 **Sol Soler** Plaça del Sol, 21

8 **Pepa Tomate** Plaça de la Revolució, 17

9 **La Xula Taperia** C. de la Mare de Deu dels Desamparats, 18

10 **La Vermuteria del Tano** Carrer de Joan Blanques, 17

11 **Bar Bodega Quimet** Carrer de Vic, 23

12 **Bar Roble** Carrer de Luis Antúnez, 7

13 **L'Anxoveta** Carrer de Sant Domènec, 14-16

▸ 14 **La Pepita** Carrer de Còrsega, 343 (p. 26)

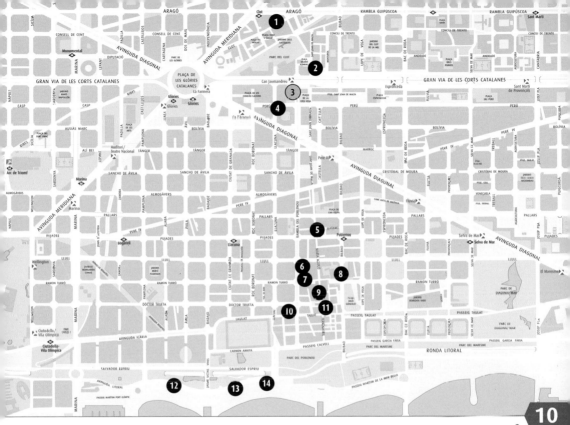

10

SANT MARTÍ

Barcelona

© Triangle Postals SL

© Foreword:
Joan Barril

© Recipes:
Amanda Laporte

© Texts:
Josep Liz

© Photography:
Jordi García
Iñaki Aldrey (p. 38)

© Maps:
Triangle Postals SL

Editorial direction: Ricard Pla
Editor: Josep Liz
Coordination: Paz Marrodán
Translation: Mark Waudby
Graphic design: David Martínez
Printed by: C. ESTELAR 2-2018
Printed in Barcelona
Registration number: Me 352-2014
ISBN: 978-84-8478-596-5

Acknowledgements:
Sofia Boixet, José María Parrado, Jordi Vilà, Marc Cuenca,
José Luis Cánovas, Jordi Cruz, Joan Martínez, Mónica de la Torre,
Francesc Tort, Carles Abellan, Joan Carles Ninou, Josep Maria Solé,
Manuel Simoes, Toni Simoes, Kim Díaz, Julián Fernández,
María Fernández, Albert Adrià, Quimet Pérez, Juan Carlos Iglesias,
Antonio Betorz, Bar Mut, Bodega 1900, Cañete barra y mantel,
Casa de Tapas Cañota, El Tomás de Sarrià, El Velódromo,
El Xampanyet-Ca l'Esteve, Els Tres Porquets, Fàbrica Moritz,
Gran Bodega Saltó, La Cova Fumada, La Pepita, La Taverna del Clínic,
La Vinya del Senyor, Lolita Taperia, Mundial Bar, Quimet & Quimet,
Taktika Berri, Tapas 24, Ten's Tapas Restaurant.

Triangle Postals, SL
Sant Lluís, Menorca
Tel. +34 971 15 04 51
triangle@triangle.cat
www.triangle.cat

TRIANGLE▼BOOKS